Managing the Delight Factor

James J. Lynch

IFS International Limited, UK
1993

James J. Lynch, a consultant on customer care and business ethics, is managing partner of Service Excellence Associates. He has devised 'The Integrity Audit', which is used by leading European companies. He is the author of seven books, including *Ethical Banking* and *The Psychology of Customer Care*.

Details of consultancy and training services on managing the Delight Factor are available from:

Service Excellence Associates
4 Moor Terrace
Talbot Road
Hawkhurst
Kent TN18 4PF
United Kingdom

Telephone/Fax: (0580) 753651

British Library Cataloguing-in-Publication Data

A catalogue record for this book is available from the British Library.

ISBN: 1-85907-000-0

© **1993 IFS International Limited,** Wolseley Business Park, Kempston, Bedford MK42 7PW, UK.

Photo-typeset by A J Latham Ltd., Houghton Regis, Dunstable, UK.

Printed by Bell & Bain, Glasgow, Scotland.

For my grandchildren,
Eleanor, Emma and Oscar,
who are sources of delight

CONTENTS

Chapter 5: The Delight Makers

Chapter 6: Managing the Hedonistic Experience

Chapter 7: Nudging into Delight

Chapter 8: Creating a Sense of Delight

Chapter 9: Managing the Delight Factor

Chapter 10: The Seven Secrets of the Delight Factor

Preface

Most people are hedonists, each seeking pleasure in a myriad of ways. A few may be sybaritic, living solely for pleasure, but the majority acknowledge that life is a blend of pleasure, pain and tedium. The demands of everyday life require the performance of tasks which are wearisome, boring and time consuming. Many of these tasks relate to our role as customers. This book is about reducing the element of tedium in the lives of customers and transforming it into pleasure. The mechanism for achieving this is the Delight Factor.

The growing awareness among manufacturers and service industries of the strategic importance of quality and customer care is narrowing the customer service differentiation between competitors. While there is still much scope for improvement, there is little to choose between the service leaders in such industries as airlines, banks, hotels, supermarkets, and public utilities.

As market and political pressures spur on the laggards to enhance service quality levels or go to the wall, the pressure on the service leaders increases. In addition, consumer-biased legislation, industry wide customer service codes and other consequences of the 'Customer Revolution' have made consumers more discerning and more demanding – expectation levels have been raised and good customer service is now taken for granted. The issue facing service leaders in all industries is how to keep ahead of customers' expectations and outmatch the competition. This is where the Delight Factor comes into play.

The Delight Factor is the agent for creating in customers a sense of fulfilment which goes beyond satisfaction. It shapes and transforms customers' perceptions of quality and care; enhances their experience as seekers of solutions to their problems;

deepens their sense of being served; and enables them to make optimum use of their time. There is nothing mysterious about the Delight Factor, but its effect can be magical – surprising the sceptic and enchanting the wary. Basically, it is the provision of a level of customer care which transcends what is current best practice in any service industry.

Service quality is cerebral, using brain power to optimise service delivery systems. Customer care is emotional, seeking to create good feelings. The Delight Factor is spiritual, releasing a sense of uplift. Those who are not imbued with the spirit of delight cannot endow others with it. Whereas conventional customer care can operate from the standpoint of the carer, delight is the outcome of a symbiosis of interdependency between carer and customer. The Delight Factor is not a package of customer service practices which can be applied cosmetically to provide a mask of care, hiding a reality of indifference; it is a philosophy which has to be adopted systemically, permeating all parts of a company and transforming its soul as well as its outward appearance.

This book aims at helping all engaged in customer care to provide an endless range of Delight Factors which will sustain differentiation in a way that conventional approaches to customer care have not been able to achieve. It begins with a critique of these conventional approaches before moving on to redefining the concept of the customer.

The 'New Customer' seeks solutions, time and delight, not only in terms of physical and psychological needs, but also the satisfaction of spiritual needs. At the core of the book there is guidance on how to release the spirit of customer care.

When is comes to giving pleasure, there is much which the providers of entertainment and leisure pursuits can teach the providers of more mundane services. An analysis of 'the delight makers' in such hedonistic or pleasure-giving industries as the arts, the media, sports and tourism reveals a five-step approach to evoking the Delight Factor which can be adapted to any service industry.

Managing the hedonistic experience of customers calls for new areas of competence at all levels, so that satisfaction can be transformed into delight. Shifting from satisfaction to delight need not necessarily require greater effort or more sophisticated techniques. Often what is needed is simply a nudge. In the chapter 'Nudging into Delight' there are details of around 60 nudges which can be used in managing the Delight Factor.

The roles of the senses and emotions in creating a sense of delight is the subject of Chapter 8. Detailed guidance is given on such topics as appealing to the senses and ways of providing emotional support to customers.

What we are encountering in the 1990s is an entirely new field of management – 'Experience Management'. This book provides an insight into what this new management discipline calls for in all types of organisations, ranging from airlines to banks and from department stores to hotels. More importantly, it shows how to practice 'Experience Management' in practical down-to-earth ways. Only when our feet are firmly on the ground will we feel able to release this new spirit of customer care.

James J. Lynch
Lions Green
East Sussex

Chapter 1

Beyond Service Quality

Introduction

W hen quality service is commonplace and prices are equal, how can you steal a march on the competition? When regulatory bodies and consumer groups define service standards, how can you differentiate your customer care? When customers take continuously improving quality for granted, how can you keep giving them pleasant surprises? The answer lies in the 'Delight Factor' – the capacity to provide customers with experiences that transcend the normal standards of quality service.

The 1980s witnessed a dawning of the awareness of quality service as a strategic weapon in the fight for market growth and profitability. The service sector, from airlines to zoos, set about finding ways to enhance customer satisfaction. Myriad quality improvement programmes were launched to make 'Service Providers' more responsive to customer needs. Surliness gave way to smiles; broken promises were replaced by 'Customer Contracts'; haphazard performance was banished by clearly defined service standards and measures. The customer was swiftly made the centre of attention in business planning and company operations.

Unfortunately for many companies, the heightening of their customers' awareness of quality service also increased customer sensitivity to poor service. A decreasing tolerance for inept service provision was compounded by expectations of enhanced service delivery. Seeking ways of responding to these pressures, service companies tended to adopt and adapt the quality philosophy and practices of manufacturing companies commonly known as Total Quality Management (TQM). That was their first mistake.

The Pitfalls of TQM

TQM is an excellent philosophy for any company engaged in the manufacture of products. It is a process designed to ensure that everyone in a company is committed to eliminating errors and waste by ensuring that all activities are carried out right first time, every time.

At the centre of any TQM system lie a number of processes, particularly statistical process control, flow charting, sampling, and quality circles. Properly applied, TQM can not only enhance product reliability, but also boost morale and increase profitability by reducing costs. The spread of TQM has been spurred on by the imposition of conformance to international quality standards as a condition of receiving contracts to supply governments, public utilities and a growing number of major companies. In particular, the International Standards Organisation (ISO) Standard 9000 Series defines how best to design and operate a TQM system:

- *ISO 9000* – provides guidelines on the selection and use of quality management and quality assurance standards.

- *ISO 9001* – provides quality system models for design/ development, production, installation and servicing.

- *ISO 9002* – defines quality methodologies applicable to production and installation.

- *ISO 9003* – defines quality methodologies for final inspec- tion and testing.

- *ISO 9004* – provides guidelines on the elements of quality management and systems.

Armed with these standards, manufacturers can develop

quality manuals which adapt the ISO 9000 series to their specific products and processes. Likewise, those engaged in service industries can adapt TQM techniques to their administrative systems. But as we shall see, over-reliance on such techniques can be dangerous in a service environment. Even in manufacturing there are a number of pitfalls to TQM:

- It is a *panacea* for all a company's problems: over-reliance on such techniques as a cure for poor supervision and mismanagement can lead to disillusionment with the TQM philosophy.

- Inculcating the philosophy and introducing the quality systems is a longer-term commitment of management resources than is usually recognised. This can lead to frustration and taking short-cuts which devalue the benefits of the TQM approach.

- The realisation of the need for continuous improvement can have an adverse affect on morale, particularly if success is not adequately recognised and rewarded.

TQM shares these problems with management philosophies, such as 'Management by Objectives' and performance appraisal, which have waxed and waned in popularity over the years. However, the pitfalls increase when over zealous proponents of TQM transfer the approach from manufacturing to the service sector. The reasons for this are as follows:

- In manufacturing, the customer is concerned only with the outcome (the product). In service industries the customer is involved in the process as well as being concerned with the outcome.

- In manufacturing, customer satisfaction is determined by the functioning of the product: does it conform as specified? In service industries, customer satisfaction depends as much on psychological factors as on performance of a tangible product (if one exists).

- Whereas products are often standardised, every service experience is unique for the customer, varying in time, mood, urgency and even place.

Any quality system in a service industry needs to be designed to cater for the customer's needs, both physically and psychologically. This means that quality standards need to be capable of defining the desired performance characteristics, while at the same time permitting deviations from the standards in order to delight the customer.

Preconditions for Delight

Delight is a physiological state of temporary pleasure, a thing of the spirit, radiating from the person experiencing it. Delight can transform a situation and change perceptions. Delight is more than satisfaction, because the latter is the result of expectations and needs being met, while the former is the result of exceeding expectations by meeting needs in a surprising way. In effect, delight is the spiritual essence of customer care, and the extent to which we can free that spirit is dependent on our ability to manage the Delight Factor.

For the Delight Factor to come into play a number of conditions need to be met:

- There must be a solid infrastructure in the form of a quality service system.
- The concept of the customer must be redefined.
- The context in which the customer experiences service must be looked at afresh.
- Customers' perceptions need to be shaped.
- Management must recognise the importance of process as well as outcome in the training and direction of staff.

These preconditions are covered in detail in subsequent chapters. However, a few comments on each will help to set the scene.

Establishing the infrastructure for a quality service system provides a solid foundation for the standards and practices on which a company can build its reputation for customer care. Without such a foundation, services will be at the very best volatile, and the chances of evoking delight will certainly be remote. Management by serendipity does not provide a secure base for winning and keeping customers. Delight should not be left to the vagaries of chance if it is to be part of a strategic armoury.

Aiming the Delight Factor at the right target requires re-thinking the shape and desires of that target – the customer. Over the years, the labels used by different service industries have created mind-sets in both customer and provider which need to be challenged. The danger of stereotyping customers needs to be recognised; we must make a fresh start and look at customers' needs across a broad front. The view of the customer as simply a 'buyer' is outmoded: he or she is a 'seeker' looking for the satisfaction of psychological and spiritual needs as well as more prosaic and physical ones.

The extent to which such needs can be satisfied is largely dependent on the context in which the service is delivered. By varying the context, it is possible to add value to the customer's experience at minimal cost. For example, in transforming time spent queuing from a chore into a period for entertainment or self-improvement, the context changes the customer's perception although the reality from the provider's viewpoint is unchanged. Context and perception are inter-dependent phenomena. The more varied the context, the greater will be the opportunities to shape customers' perceptions. Modern technology provides endless possibilities for changing the context of service delivery.

The word 'delivery' helps to remind us that service is a process as well as an outcome. As service outcomes, such as meals, journeys or financial assistance, become more standardised, it will increasingly be the process that determines the extent to which a customer is satisfied: it is in the process that there will be opportunities to delight.

The Realm of Delight

In the world of the emotions, delight is a realm bordered by satisfaction on one side and ecstasy on the other. This book shows how we can help customers to cross the boundary from satisfaction to delight. The crossing of the other boundary is beyond our scope. Sexual bliss, entrancing scenery or exquisite music, can cause us to move into the state of ecstasy; but only we can open *that* border gate by willingly giving ourselves to the embrace of an intense experience.

At the boundary between satisfaction and delight, things are more orderly. It is the provider of services who stands at the crossing point. For some, their role is perceived as that of guard blocking entry to experiences that delight; for others their role is that of a guide who makes the journey from satisfaction to delight easier and more enjoyable than would otherwise be the case.

This book is, in sense, a Baedeker for those who seek the role of guide in the little explored realm of delight. It maps out the best routes for different types of service industry, and advises on the skills and equipment needed to get the greatest benefit from each part of the domain, whether sensual or emotional; it warns against the physical and psychological pitfalls which lie in wait for the unwary traveller. Above all, it helps to plot new routes for those who seek to steal a march on their competitors.

We have seen earlier in this chapter that the 1980s saw the beginning of an era of 'Assured Quality'. As the benefits of TQM spread and increase the quality awareness in customers, we are moving into an era of 'Assumed Quality'. The very success of quality initiatives carries in its wake the flotsam of complacency. Customers expect satisfaction, and assume that quality systems have been installed, and that their needs will be met, and their expectations fulfiled. In due course, guarantees of satisfaction will in themselves become blunt instruments in the fight for service quality leadership.

For both manufacturing and service companies, the era of 'Assumed Quality' will offer new challenges and opportunities. Staff will have to be motivated to accept a regime of continuous quality improvement. Customers will need greater compensation, both psychological and financial, when assumed standards of performance are not met. Continuous improvement is, by definition, not an achieving process – for its goal is never reached. It is rather a striving process, in which achievement comes from continuing to strive. The Delight Factor has a pivotal role in sustaining the will to strive. It transports both customer and service provider together into a state beyond mere satisfaction. It brightens the mundane, sharpens perceptions, and exceeds expectations.

Like any other voyage of discovery, crossing from satisfaction to delight requires careful planning, sometimes blazing new trails, and always employing well-equipped guides.

Characteristics of Delight

The Delight Factor is a conceptual vehicle which enables the provider of a service to give customers an experience of enhanced enjoyment which is beyond simple satisfaction. The experience can be in the domains of the senses or of the emotions, both of which are to be found in the realm of delight.

Delight has the following characteristics:

- It is a state which is inhabited in short time spans.
- It provides countless opportunities for pleasant surprises.
- Entry to it rarely happens by accident.
- No two journeys in it are exactly the same.
- All incursions into delight need to be managed.

A customer's stay in the realm of delight may last a fleeting moment or several hours, but seldom longer. This is because it makes demands on the senses and emotions which are difficult to sustain over a long period. The pleasure of the tickle becomes pain if continued – so too with delight. 'Little and often', rather than 'occasional and extended', should be the aim of those guiding the customer across the satisfaction/delight border.

In exploring the territory of delight the explorer can uncover countless opportunities to enhance the enjoyment of the customer through some element of surprise. In each of the domains – the senses and the emotions – there are many ways to add value to the customer's experience, both physically and psychologically. Surprise requires going beyond the expected, which means that those who seek to surprise must be aware of the customer's initial expectations. In terms of customer care, a series of small surprises is preferable to the occasional large one. This is due to the fact that setting the scene for a large surprise carries with it the possibility of a 'leak', resulting in the loss of competitive advantage.

In terms of customer care, entry into the realm of delight rarely happens by accident: if the customer makes the journey alone, the provider of customer care can claim no role. Furthermore, in such circumstances where the customer, unknown to the service provider, is delighted, there will be no feed-back to enable the latter to benefit others. This lack of feed-back can lure the guide into dangerous areas of pseudo-delight. 'Everyone enjoys this' can be a claim which is rapidly repudiated by those led down a false trail.

Delight is experienced in different ways by different people. What captivates one individual may have no effect on another, and what attracts one can repel another. Fortunately, as in any other realm, there are in delight certain routes more popular than others. Those who aspire to be guides to delight need to familiarise themselves with well-worn paths before venturing into the unknown. As long as they are aware that different routes will appeal to different people, they will avoid the trap of uniformity.

However long or short the incursion, the Delight Factor needs to be managed. This means:

- Setting realistic targets of achievement.
- Ensuring that all the skills and equipment required for the journey are on board.
- Preparing the 'passengers' to play their role in making the journey a success.
- Using the experience to improve subsequent journeys.

The transition from satisfaction to delight may last moments, but it requires long periods of preparation. There are no short-cuts. We are psychologically incapable of moving instantly from a state of dissatisfaction to one of delight without experiencing some degree of satisfaction *en route*.

The experience of delight is no accident, but rather the result of tapping into the mix of emotions and senses which combine to provide a customer with the feeling of living in a better world, a world where customer care is a reality rather than a mere aspiration. Those engaged in bringing about that reality can take hope from the fact the world is going their way when it comes to exploring the domains of the emotions and senses.

The Domain of the Emotions

In contrast to earlier generations, there is now an increasing acceptance of public displays of emotion in Western society. The reasons for this greater tolerance for 'letting it all hang out' combine medical discoveries, social trends and the impact of television.

The statue of man as 'the thinker' has been toppled and replaced by man as the feeler. The power of the emotions in influencing customer preferences is leading service industries to seek out ways in which they can use the 'emotional edge' as a competitive weapon. People engaged in service industries need to be much more knowledgeable about the emotional make-up of their customers than their predecessors.

In Chapter 8 we will explore the domain of the emotions, identifying those which must be nurtured and sustained if we are to engender feelings of delight. Emotional support is an essential skill for anyone engaged in customer care. While some individuals will find it easier than others to acquire and display the skill, all whose role it is to serve others need to be able to identify the emotional needs of their customers and respond accordingly.

The Domain of the Senses

In contrast to the many emotions which can be brought into play when experiencing delight, there are only five senses: sight, smell, taste, hearing and touch.

Although limited in number, the senses can be limitless in their intensity. As the number of senses which are acted upon in a pleasurable experience increase, the greater the delight. As with the emotions, those who are involved in customer care must be competent in stimulating and managing the senses. How the necessary competence can be acquired, and applied in order to heighten a sense of delight, is covered in Chapter 8.

The Emergence of Delight

There are a number of social trends which account for the growing realisation of the importance of the Delight Factor in attracting and retaining customers. First among these is an increasing awareness of interconnections between mind, body and spirit in providing customer care. Another trend is the recognition that a holistic approach is needed to enable individuals to cope with their triple role as consumer/ citizen/producer. In each of these roles the fillip of pleasure engendered by delight makes it easier to respond to their sometimes conflicting demands.

Acknowledging accountability not only for one's own life, but for safeguarding the lives of future generations, means that as customers we bring a far wider range of criteria to bear when making choices between competing companies. In Chapter 3 we will consider such criteria as social responsibility, environmental awareness, and ethnic sensitivity. It would be foolish to ignore the traditional influences of choice such as price, reliability and durability. But when there is little to differentiate these criteria among rival firms, the customer will refer to other factors, not least of which will be delight.

The Competence to Delight

Six clusters of competence are needed in managing the Delight Factor. Mention already has been made of two – emotional support and sensual stimulation – to which must be added:

- Anticipation of needs.
- Expectations gate-keeping.
- Perception shaping.
- Time care.

Managers will need, in addition to these, four other competences:

- Trend scanning.
- Opportunity mapping.
- Evangelism.
- Empowerment.

These will be described in detail in Chapter 6.

Conclusion

Awareness of the importance of TQM and customer care in attracting and retaining consumers took a quantum leap in the 1980s. Although there remains much scope for improvement in standards of service in many industries, those who have pioneered quality initiatives have created the assumption among their customers that satisfaction is guaranteed. The competitive advantage of the path-finders is being eroded as more and more companies reach the frontier of zero defects.

A new frontier beckons: quality care that delights. As we progress through the 1990s, market leadership will pass to those who have laid claim to the high ground of delight. The skillful use of the Delight Factor will become the new basis for influencing customer choice. However, before a company can transport its customers into the realm of delight it must have secured its position in the battlefields of customer satisfaction. It is to the mastery of these fields of battle that we now turn.

Chapter 2

The New Customer

Introduction

The term 'New Customer' is more than a stylish label; it signals a shift in the values which are influencing customer behaviour. In the 1990s, customers bring to the point of purchase concerns and needs which go beyond the traditional focus on price and quality. Indeed, both these words need to be thought of differently. 'Price' can no longer be looked on as a purely economic phenomenon, a financial sacrifice a customer is willing to make when purchasing a product or service – social, environmental and psychological costs now come into the price calculation. Similarly, 'quality' is not judged solely on the physical attributes of a product or service; psychic and environmental value come into play in assessments of quality.

Above all, the concept of the 'customer' needs to be redefined. Simply accepting 'customer' as a synonym for 'buyer' is outmoded and misleading. Today, the 'customer' seeks three things:

- Solutions.
- Time.
- Delight.

They motivate all customer behaviour. Ways of redefining the customer are shown in Table 2.1.

Seeking Solutions

When we have a problem, we set out to find a solution, either on our own or with the help of others. In the latter case we

— 13 —

TABLE 2.1
REDEFINING THE CUSTOMER

Traditional Role	Actual Role	Needs		
		Physical	Psychological	Spiritual
Patient.	Health seeker.	– Medical/surgical treatment leading to a cure.	– Reassurance. – Confidence. – Understanding.	– Holistic approach to improving mind and body. – New horizons of opportunity through a new lease of life.
Passenger.	Safe arrival seeker.	– Punctual arrival at desired destination.	– Assurance of reliability. – Relaxation.	– Respect for local/global environment.
Shopper.	Provisions seeker and/or self-image reinforcer.	– Provisions. – Clothes. – Furniture. – Personal Services.	– Reliability. – Enhanced self-esteem. – Competence.	– Confirmation of identity. – Contributor to improved eco-system
Theatre goer.	Entertainment seeker and/or enlightenment seeker.	– Comfort. – Enjoyable play.	– Relaxation. – Amusement. – Distraction.	– Spiritual up-lift. – Enhanced self-awareness. – Improved understanding

Cont'd.....

TABLE 2.1
REDEFINING THE CUSTOMER

Traditional Role	Actual Role	Needs		
		Physical	*Psychological*	*Spiritual*
Holiday maker.	Renewal seeker and/or relaxation seeker.	– Accommodation. – Travel. – Entertainment. – Appropriate weather. – Exercise.	– Relaxation. – Leisure.	– Renewal of total energy. – Enhanced relationships. – Positive self-image.
Borrower.	Financial aid seeker.	– Loan.	– Advice. – Understanding.	– Faith in own judgement.
Investor.	Financial growth seeker.	– Savings options. – Investment options.	– Security. – Competence. – Sound advice.	– Contributor to a better world order. – Enhanced self-worth.
Hotel Guest.	Accommodation and nourishment seeker.	– Accommodation for personal or business use. – Food and drink. – Conference and leisure facilities.	– Competence. – Reliability.	– Staff not exploited. – No opulence surrounded by misery of under-class.

assume the role of customer – exchanging what we possess for what we want. Problems come in many forms, ranging from 'What shall we have for dinner?' to 'How do I get from London to New York in the shortest possible time?' Whatever the problem, it will fall into one of three categories:

* Life maintaining.
* Life enhancing.
* Life changing.

Day in, day out, we seek solutions to problems connected with surviving. Many of these, such as what to eat, how to keep clean, how to travel to and from work, are recurring and can be labelled as *quotidian*. Quotidian problems are often perceived as chores, things we would rather not do. Therefore, as customers we seek to:

* Get others to perform them for us.
* Reduce the frequency with which they must be performed.
* Automate the tasks involved.
* Bundle together a number of chores.
* Eliminate the chore.

Historically, the role of servants was to perform chores on behalf of their masters and mistresses. Many of these chores related to food and hygiene. Seeds had to be planted, crops garnered and stored, food prepared and meals served. People and their clothes needed to be kept clean, rooms dusted, beds changed and dirt removed. This long association of 'chores' with 'service' still influences perceptions of service as a servile act rather than a life enriching one. In today's world the individual servant tied to one household has been largely replaced by 'service agencies' dealing with chores such as laundering or food preparation on a large, impersonal scale. However, as we shall see, there is an increasing desire on the part of many customers for a personalisation of the impersonal. This manifests itself in the use of first names, home deliveries, and the provision of 'optional extras' which enable the customer to put a personal stamp on the product or service.

Durability and reliability have made chores easier. Longer lasting necessities from light bulbs to car tyres extend the period between replacements. 'Long life' foods, concentrated detergents and perpetual batteries all reduce the chore of replenishment. Likewise, shopping by telephone, television, or fax, dilutes the chore of queuing and frustration of finding goods out of stock.

There are certain chores which cannot be delegated nor automated completely, such as hairdressing or surgery. Nevertheless, it is possible to have a manicure/pedicure simultaneously with a haircut and treatments for more than one ailment can be performed on a single hospital visit. Such bundling or 'time-layering' plays an increasing role in making chores more acceptable to customers.

Ideally, we would be delighted to eliminate all chores, and real advances are being made. Self-cleaning ovens, fully prepared food and permanent shining floors are all examples of chore-eliminating products. Advances in medicine, security systems and meal preparation are examples of areas where service industries are striving to reduce and eliminate tasks which now occupy their customers' time.

The second category of needs for which as customers we seek solutions are those which we consider to be life enhancing; things that make us feel good – sweeteners of life. Obviously, personal circumstances and preferences play a large part in shaping our concept of the desirable. Holidays, theatre outings, family celebrations and buying what we consider luxuries are all contributors to the good life. Those whose job it is to cater for these needs must be sensitive to the threat of undesired intrusions into enjoyment sought by their customers. In particular, attention has to be paid to:

- Recognising that all life enhancing needs are discretionary.

- Ensuring that the pacing of activities is appropriate to the customer's needs.
- Providing a range of options to make the event 'special'.

One person's luxury may be another's necessity, but the distinction nevertheless exists in the mind of every customer. Customers have to be enticed into satisfying their life enhancing needs in a particular way. The purchase of a new car may have to vie with the installation of a swimming pool, and a visit to the theatre with the purchase of the latest 'best seller'. The psychological dimension looms larger in life enhancement than it does in life maintenance, and choice is greatly influenced by a desired self-image. Whereas, the satisfaction of life maintenance needs governs what we *must do* to survive, satisfying life enhancement needs governs what we *can do* to make life more pleasant.

This is why the pacing of life enhancing services is so important. When faced with a chore our aim is to deal with it very swiftly, when it comes to a pleasurable experience we want to enjoy if for as long as the pleasure can be sustained. The rushed celebratory dinner and the over-long film are examples of failures in pleasure pacing. The process requires as much if not more attention than the outcome when it comes to meeting life enhancement needs.

By their nature, life enhancing events are escapes from the humdrum of daily existence. They are perceived in anticipation as 'special'. Often they are occasions when individuals want to be 'taken out of themselves', metaphorically transported to another world. Life enhancing need fulfilment allows great scope for the Delight Factor to operate. The pleasuring of the psyche is pivotal to success in life enhancement.

The psyche also looms large in the finding of solutions to life changes. This category of needs encompasses all activities associated with events which have a significant impact on the life of a customer. Ranging from life stages such as birth, marriage and death, to career changes, house changes or starting a business – these turning points carry with them a variety of problems which customers need help in resolving. When seeking to solve them, the service provider needs to be mindful of:

- The common/unique experience.
- The aureole effect.
- Mis-matched paradigms.

The common/unique experience appears at first sight to be a contradiction: how can something be common and yet unique? The answer is that for an individual undergoing an event for the first time it is a unique experience, although it has been shared by others. The most obvious example is that of becoming a parent for the first time. Another common example is someone's first experience of flying. Despite the knowledge that literally millions of people have had a similar experience, for the first-timer it is a unique event. This needs to be borne in mind by those responsible for providing an experience which is for them an everyday occurrence.

Another feature of life changes is that around the core need which the customer is striving to meet there are clusters of other needs which are shaping the customer's perception. Just as in medieval paintings the artist would surround the head of a saintly figure with an aureole of gold to catch the attention of the viewer, so too is it necessary for the service provider to look at the total scene, and not simply the core problem. For example, purchasing a new house may be the core need of a customer, but it is surrounded by other concerns such as adjusting to new neighbours, finding schools, doctors and so forth.

Life change needs do not come singly, but in patterns; finding solutions requires the ability to recognise the paradigm. Much mutual dissatisfaction can arise when the service provider responds to a different pattern from that which is perceived by the customer. What the service provider perceives as a mere administrative hiccup, the customer may see as a major threat to completing the deal.

By thinking of the customer as a seeker we can gain a deeper insight into his or her needs. Having seen that the *process* which all customers seek is problem-solving we now turn to the one which everyone seeks more of – time.

Seeking Time

The 'New Customer' seeks not only solutions to problems, but also ways to make better use of time. Life is tiny bits of time out of which each of us shapes our unique mosaic of living. A customer care challenge of the 1990s is to help customers shape their time in a pattern which optimises their satisfaction. This requires service providers to conceptualise time as a resource, as well as a measure and a psychological process. There is nothing new in such a concept *per se*; what is new is to look on time as a dimension of every product or service which we buy. It is a key dimension in determining not only customer choice, but also customer satisfaction and, therefore, repeat business.

We have seen that customers seek solutions to three categories of life problems: maintenance, enhancement and change. At any point in time, we are preoccupied with satisfying one or more of these needs. They create mind-sets which influence the amount of time which we are willing to allocate to the pursuit of satisfaction. Generally speaking, as customers, we are willing to devote more time to satisfying a life changing need than a life maintaining one. Thus, we become confused and dissatisfied when our bank expends more time in dealing with a small excess on an overdraft than in advising us on financing a house purchase.

Here we come to the first tip for success in customer time-shaping: identify the dominant lifetime mind-set of your customers. This is easier in some industries than others. For example, funeral directors are normally dealing with life change mind-sets; theme parks with life enhancing; and laundries with life maintaining. Things become more difficult in banks, airlines and hotels, though even here there are indicators in terms of product or service choice.

Having identified the dominant mind-set, the next step is to determine the 'Psychic Time Zone' in which the customer is operating.

Psychic Time Zones

Psychic Time Zones define the psychological boundaries of a sense of time passing which encompass related activities, events, feelings and experiences of an individual. We may mentally flit from time zone to time zone, but at any period of time we act in accordance with the demands of a dominant time zone.

There are 14 Psychic Time Zones which influence the psychology of customer care. These 14 form three inter-related clusters:

- Passage of Time Zones.
- Lifework Time Zones.
- Lifestyle Time Zones.

The 'New Customer' is becoming more sensitive to reconciling the conflicting demands stemming from these various Psychic Time Zones. A first step is, therefore, to find ways of time-shaping which will shift the balance of demand from performing boring and mundane tasks to those that yield pleasure and delight.

The subject of time-shaping is covered in detail in my book, *The Psychology Of Customer Care* (Macmillan Press UK, 1992). What follows is a resume of the main points.

Passage of Time Zones

This cluster consists of four zones within which customers experience a consciousness of the passing of time and its effect on them. In alphabetical order these zones are:

- The Biological Zone, within which we are conceived, born, grow and die.

- The Chronological Zone, within which we are conscious of the present in relation to the past and the future.
- The Durability Zone, within which we seek to extend or maintain the efficacy of the tangible.
- The Global Zone, within which we measure and synchronise the passage of time across the world. (This is a 'physical' rather than a 'psychic' time zone.)

A few illustrations of industries which cater for customer needs in each zone are:

- Food manufacturers – Biological Zone.
- Photographers – Chronological Zone.
- Dry cleaners – Durability Zone.
- Watchmakers – Global Zone.

Lifework Time Zones

This cluster also contains four related zones which we occupy in order to acquire the means necessary to maintain or enhance our standard of living. The four zones are:

- Travel.
- Work.
- Provisioning.
- Communications.

Provisioning and communications can relate to leisure as well as work, but most of us spend more time on these activities in relation to work.

The third and largest cluster is the 'Lifestyle Time Zones'; these have great potential for allowing the Delight Factor to come into play.

Lifestyle Time Zones

This cluster contains seven time zones which are defined by the choices which we make in the use of discretionary time. These choices are influenced by our value system, age and capabilities. The zones are:

- Family.
- Leisure.
- Private.
- Ritual.
- Survival.
- Waiting.
- Worship.

The 'Survival Time Zone' is that in which all our endeavours at a point in time are focused on undergoing an undesired experience with minimal adverse effect on life and limb, e.g., avoiding a car crash.

The 'Waiting Time Zone' is that in which we experience an interval between the awareness of a need and its satisfaction. Our tolerance for the duration of an interval is influenced by whether satisfaction of the need will result in life change, life enhancement, or life maintenance. Both these zones are largely determined by our lifestyle aspirations, hence their inclusion in this cluster.

The success of customer time-shaping depends on the ability of the care provider to identify the dominant time zone within which the customer is seeking satisfaction. In addition, the more time zones in which the service provider can synchronise fulfilment of needs, the higher the level of customer satisfaction will be. Airlines provide an obvious example of the need to manage synchronicity. Passengers flying across the Atlantic have needs not only in terms of travel; their biological, leisure, work and communications needs must also be catered for. Indeed, the main determinant of satisfaction may be the enjoyment of the in-flight film rather than the performance of the aircraft.

To ensure success in time-shaping, service providers need to work simultaneously on as many Psychic Time Zones as possible to enhance customer satisfaction.

Within any time zone the level of satisfaction will be influenced by the manner in which the care provider helps the customer to deal with particular time states.

Time States

These are the states of mind which are determining customer behaviour at a given point of time. Some states are positive, some negative and a few are neutral. For example, in the Biological Zone, illness results in a negative state, fitness is a positive one. In the Travel Zone, overcrowding produces a negative state, punctual arrival a positive one.

A key factor in time-shaping is to reinforce the positive time states and reduce or eliminate the negative ones. The more time states a care provider can identify and act on, the more opportunities there will be for optimising customer satisfaction. Hence the two other essentials of time-shaping:

- Reinforce positive time states.
- Eliminate negative time states.

Techniques for Customer Time-Shaping

There are at least 12 ways by which we can add value to the time dimension of goods and services:

- Compressing.
- Layering.
- Diverting.
- Smoothing.
- Substituting.

- Plexing.
- Contra-flowing.
- Extending.
- Exchanging.
- Pacing.
- Enhancing.
- Signalling.

A word on some of these:

Layering is enabling the customer to experience more than one time zone simultaneously. The earlier airline example shows how this can be done.

Substituting is undertaking for payment an activity which would otherwise occupy the time of an individual. This can range from using an estate agent to employing a butler.

Plexing is providing a product or service which satisfies customers in different time zones. Hotels, for example, may be providing the same meals for different guests, some of whom are celebrating a family event, some engaged in business negotiations and others who are on vacation.

The nature of the customer need will determine the selection of the time-shaper. The more time-shapers a care provider can use, the more effective he/she will be in competing *with* time.

While selecting appropriate time-shapers may call for some in-depth market research, we can easily identify time mis-shapers.

Customer Time Mis-Shaping

There are five ways to reduce customer satisfaction through time mis-shaping:

- *Wasting time* through mistakes and delays.

- *Killing time* through lack of options for spending it.
- *Warping time* by forcing customers into an inappropriate time zone – for example, an emergency landing by an aircraft, food poisoning after a meal.
- *Interrupting time,* thus causing an undesired change in time zone or state for a short period.
- *Time-jacking* by drawing the customer into an undesired time zone for a long period.

The 'New Customer' is less tolerant and forgiving when time mis-shaping occurs.

People are increasingly 'time conscious'. The reasons for this range from the advent of a new millennium (a first experience for *everyone* on earth) to advances in the speed and sophistication of telecommunications. Faced with ever-increasing options in using an ever-decreasing personal resource, we seek new ways of stemming the erosion of our being, and of shaping our time in ways which we find most satisfying. In the final analysis every product, every service has a time dimension. As standards of customer care rise in response to consumer demand, companies need to seek ways of differentiating themselves. There is no better way to go forward than to show that we care for people by caring for their time. By so doing we will help them experience the feeling we all seek – delight.

Film making is, perhaps, the leading hedonistic industry, though not all its products give delight. A time-shaping analysis of how a film can be used to give delight in a number of Psychic Time Zones is given in Table 2.2.

Traditionally, a film could be enjoyed only in a cinema and in only one Psychic Time Zone – that of leisure. The advent of television opened up opportunities to experience the delights of a film at home, either in the Family Time Zone or privately. This greatly increased scope for time layering. Family meals can be taken while viewing, to name but one alternative activity. Research reveals that other activities undertaken while viewing range from knitting to having sex.

TABLE 2.2
THE FILM – AN EXAMPLE OF TIME-SHAPING

Traditional Psychic Time-Zone	New Psychic Time-Zone	
	Mode	**Zone**
Leisure.	– First Release.	– Leisure plus -.
	– Aircraft/Cruise Ship.	– Travel.
	– Video Cassette Sales.	– Provisioning (Gift).
	– Video Rental.	– Family/Private.
	– Pay Television.	– Family/Private.
	– Television (General).	– Family/Private.
	Other Possibilities	
	– Television at Christmas/Easter.	– Ritual.
	– Advertising Products.	– Provisioning.
	– Retrospective Release.	– Chronological.
	– Book Tie-in.	– Private.
	– Record Tie-in.	– Family/Private.
	– Training Courses.	– Work.
	– Product Tie-in.	– Provisioning.
	– Theme-park Attraction.	– Chronological.

When the video cassette recorder came into existence it further extended the time-shaping options for the film industry. Videos of films could be used to off-set the tedium of journeys by coach, train, ferry as well as aircraft. A cherished movie could be given as a present. Delight, especially for young customers, could be evoked, not only by a visit to the cinema, but by 'spin-offs' such as clothes, toys, books and posters.

Today the profitability of a film is often more dependent on video and TV sales than on box office earnings in the traditional Leisure Time Zone. The example of a film can be replicated by other industries which use time-shaping as a means of extending opportunities for profit enhancement through strategic use of the Delight Factor. The question that brought about marketing revolutions in the 1960s was 'What business are we in?'. In the 1990s the clue to successful marketing is: 'In what Psychic Time Zones can we delight the customer?'.

Seeking Delight

In addition to solutions to problems and time-shaping, there is a third cluster of needs. These stem from the 'New Customer's' wish to have good feelings and to experience delight. Delight is a state in which we feel good about ourselves and the situation we are in. While delight can not be produced to order, it can be stimulated, and the conditions created for its emergence in the mind and heart of the customer.

The characteristics of delight are that:

- It is a temporary state which needs frequent replenishing.
- It can be experienced both psychologically and physically.
- It is observable.
- It can be reinforced by being shared.

Habituation is the enemy of delight; getting used to a stimulus so that we no longer react to it kills off the Delight Factor inherent in the stimulus. It is therefore necessary to identify a wide range of sources of delight.

The major sources of delight can be classified under seven headings:

- Achievements.
- Acquisitions.
- Emotional releases.
- Sensations.
- Surprises.
- Vicarious pleasure.
- Self-fulfilment.

The successful achievement of a goal is perhaps the most common source of delight. Awareness of the goal and the ability to help the customer achieve it are essential in managing this aspect of the Delight Factor. Acknowledging the achievement can enhance the delight of the achiever. But this will only happen if the manner of acknowledgement is appropriate to the achievement, and if the bestowing of the acknowledgement is as close as possible to the time of the achievement.

The next source of delight, acquisitions, can range from a new dress to a new house. Whatever it may be, there will be tangible evidence of this source of delight. An item may be acquired after a long period of planning and saving, or it may be an impulse buy. No matter the speed at which it is acquired, if an item is to be a source of delight it must meet the following criteria:

- It is desired.
- It exceeds expectations.
- It reinforces one's positive self-image.

In terms of managing the Delight Factor, it is therefore necessary to be aware of the intensity of desire which the customer has for the item, his/her expectations, and ways in which the item is likely to boost the customer's self-image.

When it comes to emotional releases there are two sides to the Delight Factor, a positive and a negative. The positive side is a build-up and release of positive feelings of happiness; the negative is the release from actual or expected fears and anxieties. To manage the Delight Factor in these circumstances it is necessary to anticipate and empathise with the emotional profile of the customer.

The sense of touch provides both pleasurable and painful feelings. Taste guides us through a meal which may result in pleasure or sickness. Our eyes reveal new sources of delight, while our nose alerts us to pleasing fragrances or hidden dangers. Contradictory sensations such as a beautifully decorated but foul smelling house, destroy the Delight Factor. When it comes to sensations, the secret of successful management of the Delight Factor is to play to as many senses as possible, as is shown in Chapter 8.

Surprises are an important source of delight, as long as they are pleasant and not overwhelming in their impact. Depending on their nature, surprises can bewilder, shock, disconcert or baffle – there is no Delight Factor in such surprises. On the other hand, surprises that amaze, astonish, thrill, can give pleasure. For such surprises to have the desired effect, timing is of the essence. Care needs to be taken to avoid the element of surprise being lost through the premature release of information.

Delight shared can be delight greatly increased. Parents can enjoy vicarious pleasure from observing the delight of their children; the bestower of a gift can take delight in the joy of the recipient. Therefore, when managing the Delight Factor it is important to seek ways of spreading the feeling of joy beyond the individual targeted. The greater the area of 'delight fall-out' the higher the levels of satisfaction.

Of course, there are many occasions when delight is a totally individual experience stemming from some act of self-fulfilment.

This differs from the achievement of an externalised goal; fulfilment could well be totally interiorised, making it difficult to manage the Delight Factor. The important element in such situations is to gain the confidence of the customer, encouraging openness and trust by using techniques of customer bonding. Forging close long-term relationships with customers will provide insights into their needs and expectations, their self-image and the ways in which they seek self-fulfilment.

Transforming the Mundane

Delight manifests itself in different shapes and sizes. No matter how humdrum a business may appear, it will offer opportunities to delight its customers. These opportunities will reveal themselves in various ways:

- The nature of the product or service.
- Peripherals.
- Ambience.
- Delivery systems.
- Behaviour of the providers of care.

Some products have a Delight Factor built into them. It can vary from the ingenuity of the Swiss army knife with a variety of implements combined in a small space to the electronic driver aids available in a car.

There are many ways in which the Delight Factor can be built into a product, among these are:

- Individuality.
- Ingenuity.
- Flexibility.
- Mobility.

- Ease of use.
- Durability.

Individuality is the 'Just for you' promise which delights. In an age of mass production, customers seek products which have an appearance of individuality if not uniqueness. The more exclusive the product, the greater its propensity to delight, since the owner appreciates its exclusivity. Labels which proclaim that the product is available to a select few are as prized as the product itself. Hence, the spread of designer clothes brandishing the name of their designer or manufacturer.

Ingenuity by capturing the imagination, in product design or use, provides a Delight Factor. This is particularly true in the case of products which perform routine functions such as cleaning and cooking. A sleek vacuum cleaner helps to glamourise a chore or a self-cleaning oven obviates it completely.

Flexibility in product use can provide a Delight Factor by enabling a number of functions to be performed simultaneously. Combining a telephone with an answer phone or a facsimile machine which can also be used for photocopying are two examples. Televisions which can be used to transact 'home banking' as well as provide entertainment have potential for more varied functions, each of which will have the capacity to delight.

Mobility, by allowing a product to be used in different locations, enhances its delight potential. Portable products of all types, ranging from camcorders to barbecues, make possible new experiences which can yield new delights.

Ease of use can be built into products. No matter how complex their function, we seek machines which are easy to use. The simpler the instructions, the more likely a piece of equipment will be the cause for delight rather than despair. This can pose dilemmas, since what is simple to use is simple to abuse. However, one way round this is to have a secret code word or number to activate the equipment. The use of Personal Identification

Numbers, pioneered by banks, is spreading into many other fields. Such devices provide a form of individuality and thus increase their own attractiveness.

Durability is an important feature of all products. It can result in delight when the product lasts longer than expected. Be it the shelf-life of food or the road-life of a car, the longer its durability, the greater its propensity to delight.

Spiritual Aspects

The 'New Customer' not only seeks delight in terms of physical and psychological needs, but also the spiritual. 'Spiritual' in this context need not be taken to mean 'religious', though religious beliefs have long influenced the choices of certain customers. Jews shun pork, no matter how cheap and well-prepared it may be; Presbyterians and other religious sects refuse to shop on Sundays; and Moslems do not drink alcohol. These are examples of the spiritual dimension at work. But its influence is not confined to members of religious sects.

In the 1990s people are increasingly seeking ways to contribute to something beyond themselves. They are aware that they have accountability for their own lives and can positively influence the lives of others. This awareness is a key attribute of the 'New Customer'. One consequence is the growing demand for alternative life styles. The 'fitness and wellness' movements are growing, resulting in a holistic approach to the combined role of consumer/citizen/producer.

There is a widening recognition of the fundamental inter-connection of body, mind, and spirit, leading to a reappraisal of traditional concepts of 'price', 'quality' and customer care. The 'New Customer' looks outwards at the consequences of each buying decision as it relates to the planet, people associated with the source of the product and the local community.

The price of a product is perceived in a variety of ways:

- Financial.
- Competitive.
- Social.
- Ecological.
- Political.

A 'cheap' car which pollutes the atmosphere is seen as expensive because of its social and ecological costs. Cheap wine produced in a country which has an oppressive regime will be spurned in favour of a more expensive product from a politically acceptable country.

Likewise with quality – 'zero defects' is considered not simply in terms of function but also in social and ecological impact. The quality of a service is also judged from a broader perspective than before. Mistakes, leading to a large mail-out correcting the error, are judged not only on the financial cost, but also in terms of the waste of trees.

The spread of spiritual values offers the service provider with both opportunity and threat. The opportunity is to broaden the basis on which customers can be made to feel good – to enjoy a sense of delight. The threat lies in companies being perceived as cynical exploiters of these new-found concerns. Spurious claims about the 'environmental friendliness' of products will result in cynical customers.

Conclusion

The 'New Customer' is a seeker of solutions, time and delight; these are the three parameters on which quality service will be judged. By helping customers find the solution to their problems and shape their time the way they want it, the chances of delighting them will greatly increase. However, the evoking of delight can no longer be left to the physical and psychological features of a product or service, the spiritual dimension must also be brought into play.

The 'New Customer' has two categories of need:

- Directed needs where others are involved.
- Self-directed needs which relate to personal circumstances.

These are listed in Table 2.3. Whatever the category, it will be seen that a greater emphasis on satisfying spiritual needs is emerging. Why this should be so and what can be done about it are the subjects of the next two chapters.

TABLE 2.3
MEETING NEEDS WITH DELIGHT

Other-Directed Needs

Type of Need	Ways of Meeting Need	Implications for the Delight Factor
Celebration – the need to signify approval and express joy to some event involving other people.	– Provision of special food and drink in abundance. – Presentation of gifts. – Wearing of special clothes.	– Enable the customer to celebrate in a manner consistent with the spirit of the event, but with distinctive characteristics which differentiates it from similar events.
Commemoration – the need to share in signified allegiance to the memory, values and beliefs associated with a past event.	– Provision of prescribed food and drink. – Presentation of mementos. – Wearing of historic clothes. – Visits to historic sites.	– Enable the customer to com-memorate the event in a manner which conveys a sense of the past and reinforces feelings of goodwill.
Confirmation – the need to have corroboration by others of your positive self-image.	– Using products which will evoke compliments. – Joining clubs of people similar to oneself. – Providing conspicuous hospitality. – Using luxury services.	– Enable the customer to project desired self-image without embarrassment.

(cont'd...)

TABLE 2.3
MEETING NEEDS WITH DELIGHT

Type of Need	Ways of Meeting Need	Implications for the Delight Factor
Other-Directed Needs		
Participation – the need to be actually or vicariously present at some event at which you enjoy the company of others.	– Attending sporting or similar event. – Attending theatrical or similar event. – Watching with others an event on TV.	– Enable the customer to participate in conditions of comfort and security which exceeds previous experiences of similar events.
Relationship Bonding – the need to establish, sustain and cement relationships of all types.	– Presentation of gifts. – Provision of hospitality. – Signifying remembrance of events significant to the other party.	– Enable the customer to achieve a desired level of contact by providing the ambience, tangibles and intangibles appropriate to the relationship.
Self-Directed Needs		
Life Change – needs relating to significant changes in life style.	– Acquiring a house. – Undergoing major surgery. – Setting up a business. – Emigrating. – Change in marital status.	– Enable the customer to satisfy need in a manner which recognises the importance of the situation and reinforces his/her self-esteem.

(Cont'd....)

TABLE 2.3
SELF-DIRECTED NEEDS

Other-Directed Needs

Type of Need	Ways of Meeting Need	Implications for the Delight Factor
Life Enhancement – needs relating to circumstances which will enhance life style and self-worth.	– Indulgence in luxury. – Impulsive gratification of a whim. – Acquiring a desired, but non-essential product. – Vacationing. – Replacing product with improved model. – Displaying increased affluence in tangible and intangible ways. – Becoming a member of an elite group.	– Enable the customer to meet the need in a manner which provides psychic added-value and assures a level of gratification higher than expected.
Life Maintaining – needs relating to sustaining ones life style without changing or enhancing it in any significant way.	– Purchasing basic foods and clothing. – Replenishing stocks. – Repairing and maintaining. – Preparing for emergencies. – Substituting higher priced goods with lower priced goods. – Bargain seeking.	– Enable the customer to satisfy need in ways which reduce chores and mask the mundane while sustaining the individual's self-esteem.

Chapter 3

The Spiritual Dimension of Customer Care

Introduction

The spiritual dimension of 'New Customer' needs has five value clusters:

- Ethical awareness.
- Economic vision.
- Ecological responsibility.
- Social sensitivity.
- Personal fulfilment.

The impact of each cluster varies between people and situations, but the service provider has to be prepared to anticipate and respond to every one of them since each provides an opportunity to evoke delight, as is shown in Table 3.1.

Ethical Awareness

Adherence to sound business ethics cannot be taken for granted. The financial frauds of recent years, typified by the Bank of Credit and Commerce International (BCCI) scandal in 1991, has strengthened the ethical awareness of customers throughout the world. Issues of life and death which formerly were the ethical province of the medical profession are now matters for public debate.

TABLE 3.1
VALUES OF THE NEW CUSTOMER

Value	Influence on Behaviour	Consequences
Ethical Awareness.	– Need for increasing reassurance on trustworthiness of service provider.	– More regulatory bodies. – Increase in customer protection legislation. – Publication of ethical codes. – Customers monitoring business conduct.
Economic Vision.	– Choice determined not only on basis of money price but on balance of economic and other values.	– Money price still important but 'value for money' is sought on a broader vision of economic advantage.
Ecological Responsibility.	– Products/services judged on their impact on the environment.	– Ecological implications of every product/service must be thought through prior to being launched.

(cont'd...)

TABLE 3.1
VALUES OF THE NEW CUSTOMER

Value	Influence on Behaviour	Consequences
Social Sensitivity.	– Purchasing influenced by social consequences for the deprived.	– Avoidance of conspicuous consumption. – Growth of services coping with social problems of inner cities, family break-up, racial tension.
Personal Fulfilment.	– Products/services which reinforce positive self-image need to be personalised.	– Increase in self-service. – Interference by service provider will be replaced with supportive interventions.

New and more powerful regulatory bodies now police most service industries; umbrella consumer rights organisations have to be listened to, and efforts made to conform to their demands. Ironically, as legislation increases, more ways of circumventing the laws are sought by the unscrupulous. Companies are increasingly being expected to articulate ethical codes which govern their conduct in dealing with customers. Although specifics will vary between industries, there are six ethical imperatives which cut across all industries and will be demanded by customers:

- Legality.
- Fairness.
- Legitimacy.
- Justification.
- Confidentiality.
- Sincerity.

Legality may at first sight appear a statement of the obvious, but with the growth of global companies it is not always obvious which law is the appropriate one when there is a dispute between customer and provider. As laws become more numerous and complex there will be an accompanying growth in litigation. Backed by consumer groups, customers will resort to claiming damages if they feel they have a grievance. The basis of grievances is likely to shift from the tangible to the intangible, from the physical to the psychological. Hedonistic damages – in broad terms, the deprivation of delight – will become the basis for a growing proportion of lawsuits by customers. Anticipating likely causes for such claims and taking preventative action to avoid them will become a key factor in customer care. Among the claims for 'hedonistic damages' could be:

- Holidays spoiled by bad weather or inadequate amenities.
- A cinema visit ruined by noisy neighbours.

- Anxiety increased by 'false alarms' on an aircraft or in hotels.
- Self-esteem damaged by the behaviour of service providers.
- Fear caused by blackout as the result of an electrical fault.
- Psychological trauma arising from witnessing an accident.

Such claims have already been made and won by customers taking action in the legal jurisdiction which is likely to give the highest compensation, most often the courts in the United States.

Concurrent with the growth of claims for hedonistic damages will be an increasing trend for governments to pass on to service providers the responsibility for customers complying with the law. An example of this is the practice of the British Government to fine airlines which carry persons who are illegal immigrants, despite the best endeavours of the airlines to check their credentials before accepting them as passengers. This assignment of legal accountability will threaten customer/ supplier relationships. Matters will become worse with the continuance in and anticipated rise in terrorism – particularly consumer terrorism which tampers with products and services in order to hold companies to ransom. Companies and their customers may be tempted to take the law into their own hands in dealing with the perpetrators of terrorism.

What at first sight may be a statement of the obvious – that it is necessary to abide by the law – becomes on analysis an overgrown part of the ethical maze which companies and customers must traverse in an increasing 'law bound', as distinct from 'law-abiding' world.

Fairness governs the terms of any transaction between buyer and seller. In all such transactions there is in the mind of each of the parties involved a 'reserve price', as in an auction. For the buyer, this is the maximum which he/she is prepared to pay to purchase the product or service; for the seller, it is the lowest price at which he/she is willing to provide the product or service. While it is unlikely that these prices will be in equilibrium, the 'New Customer' will expect a reasonable balance between the two. The financial price will not by itself determine this balance. As previously stated, other 'costs' will influence the customer's perception of a 'fair price'. Among these will be the effects of the purchase on the self-esteem of the customer, and the effect on the environment and on other segments of society, both nationally and internationally.

Fairness, like beauty, is often in the eyes of the beholder. It does not apply solely to the perceptions of the customers; service providers also need to believe that they are receiving a fair deal from their customers. The concept of 'reciprocal obligation' between customer and provider will loom large in all markets, displacing the old adage of 'buyer beware'.

Social legitimacy is that part of an ethical code which is concerned with protecting the interests of 'third parties'. Although a transaction between customer and supplier may be considered legal and fair by both parties, it is unethical if it wantonly damages the legitimate interests of others. The 'New Customer' will be on guard against those companies perceived as being predators, polluters or poachers; this trio of delight killers will be given short shrift by those who share values of ecological responsibility and social sensitivity, both of which we shall consider later in this chapter.

Justification in terms of business ethics means that a company can, if required, justify any of its policies and activities to its shareholders, employees, customers or regulatory bodies. Laws which enforce greater disclosure will be a driving force for 'justification'. But the 'New Customer' will seek conformity with the spirit of the law as well as compliance with its word. Companies which seek refuge in the law will cut themselves off from opportunities to delight their customers. A criterion of customer care will be the willingness of a company to do more for its customers than the law requires. However, this carries with it an obligation to treat all customers equitably, although not necessarily equally. Customer loyalty should carry its rewards, providing these are justifiable.

The concept of justification implies a greater openness by companies, and this could conflict with the fifth tenet of business ethics – *confidentiality*. Obviously, there are some service industries, such as finance and medicine, where the confidentiality of data on customers is of greater importance than in other sectors. However, this, like other tenets, is not simply a matter of complying with the law; it is the basis of building trust between the customer and service provider. The 'New Customer' will expect the provider to establish the nature and degree of confidentiality which he/she wants in all transactions. This could range from methods of payment to not disclosing to other customers products which the purchaser considers embarrassing. Whatever the nature of the expectation it should be respected, as long as it does not conflict with the other five tenets.

Sincerity is the last of the six values demanded by the 'New Customer'. In terms of the Delight Factor it is also the most important. Without sincerity customer care becomes 'customer con'. Permanent smiles are the curse of the demented; many customer care programmes have made them the indicators of sincerity. But genuine sincerity means keeping promises, providing the best available advice, and showing care in deed as well as word. The true spirit of sincerity has been cocooned in gimmicks and devices such as name badges and 'up-selling'. No one is suggesting that we return to the era of the scowl, the shrug of indifference, or the 'have a nice day' syndrome. But, sincerity must break out of the cocoon if it is to enable the Delight Factor to grow.

The six values which constitute ethical awareness are interdependent. Failure to practice any one of them will adversely affect the perception of the customer on all aspects of quality service. As throughout history, so in the last decade of the second millennium, ethics is a matter of deeds, not words, though without spelling out the words it is more difficult to carry out the deeds.

Economic Vision

While value-for-money will continue to be a prime concern of the 'New Customers' as of the 'old', there are other values which will be firmly within the span of their economic vision. High among these will be:

- Psychic added-value.
- Spiritual costs.
- Substitution.

Added-value can take many forms, both tangible and intangible. A product which performs several functions provides more added-value than a rival which performs only one. Versatility, flexibility, reliability, and durability are all characteristics which can bestow tangible added-value. When we turn to the intangible, the characteristics include timeliness, enhancement of self-image, improved social status, entertainment, appropriateness, and peace of mind. As the functional quality and price of products become less differentiated, psychic added-value will become more important for gaining competitive advantage. A major challenge for companies will be how to provide psychic added-value of a high order – how to delight. The beauty of psychic added-value is that, unlike its tangible twin, it need cost nothing. Putting customers at ease costs no more than making them anxious. Greeting people with a smile costs the same as greeting them with a scowl.

'Spiritual costs' have economic implications in so far as they can be a spur to or inhibitor of the purchasing decision. Many charities publish Christmas cards or have retail shops which appeal to the spirit as well as the purse. Customers are spurred on to make purchases which provide a spiritual uplift as well as economic satisfaction. Equally, the 'New Customer' will forego economic satisfaction where it is perceived that the spiritual costs associated with the purchase of a product or service are too high. The use of boycotts is not new, but it is an example of customers putting into effect their beliefs that the spiritual costs of some commodities are too high. Manufacturers and service providers will increasingly be faced with the threat of boycott and other forms of customer power if they fail to take full account of the 'New Customer's' concern for spiritual costs.

The term 'boycott' comes from the name of a harsh landowner in Ireland, Captain Boycott. In the 1880s the tenant farmers on his estate and neighbouring ones refused to deal with him, eventually forcing him to change his ways. A century later, where dealing with international issues such as apartheid in South Africa, the fur trade, animal testing of cosmetics and vivisection, customer boycotts tend to have the same characteristics regardless of the cause which has given rise to the specific action:

- Prominent companies are targeted, with one major product or service selected for sanctions. An example was the student boycott of Barclays Bank in the 1970s and 1980s because of its involvement with South Africa. The cause fuelling the boycott was the abolition of apartheid.
- The scope of the boycott is usually nation-wide rather than local, because a nationally-based retail chain is more vulnerable than a local one.
- Maximum use is made of the media by making the boycott action visually interesting and seeking headlines. In extreme cases this can lead to violence, as has occurred with animal rights activists.
- Support of well-known public personalities, particularly actors and actresses, is courted so as to give the campaign star appeal.
- Often the targeted product or service is one that is peripheral to the mainstream activity of the company being boycotted. This makes it easier for the company to comply with the demands of the boycotters, thus allowing them to claim success.

Although it is impossible for a company to avoid boycott action since it is the campaigners who select both cause and target, there should nevertheless be a boycott contingency plan which, in the event of it being targeted, will enable the company to manage the situation rather than be taken wholly unawares.

A consequence of boycotting is that the customer substitutes the targeted product or service with another. Substitution may operate for other reasons in the economic vision of the 'New Customer':

- Environmentally friendly products will replace those perceived to be environmentally hostile.
- Symbols of conspicuous consumption will give way to symbols of responsible living.
- Impulse buying will be replaced by planned gratification.

The concept of substitution acts as a link between economic vision and the next cluster of values, environmental responsibility.

Awareness of the importance of environmental issues was one of the fastest changes in social values in the 1980s. What had previously been perceived as the preoccupation of the crank was transformed into a leading priority of many individuals. Environmental responsibility will continue to be a prime concern of the 'New Customer'. There will be two streams of concern – protection of one's immediate environment, and safeguarding the environment of others. In both cases the 'New Customer' will judge companies on process as well as outcome. A consequence of this is that customers will want to be more involved in manufacturing processes, in particular the monitoring of their environmental impact. The previously mentioned 'delight killers', predators, polluters and poachers, will be stalked across the globe.

Predators plunder the underprivileged, whether disadvantaged economically, socially or politically. The 'New Customer' will be on guard against the wilful exploitation of people and natural resources. Our tolerance for 'sweated labour' becomes lower when its reality is seen on television. Those who claim that much of what appears on television is for the mindless, often overlook the role which television plays in stirring consciences. The 'New Customer' will be better informed on immoral business practices, particularly pollution and poaching.

Pollution comes in many forms: contamination of the air, poisoning of rivers, and fouling of beaches are but a few. In addition to these, more common examples, noise pollution, mind pollution, and even pollution of the spirit, are all dangers of modern living. Pollution avoidance and pollution control are two of the criteria which the 'New Customer' will weigh in the balance of choice. As with ethical awareness, compliance with the law will be seen as the minimum expected of companies with regard to their environmental impact.

Poachers are those companies which take more from the environment than they are willing to put back. Examples are the over-culling of animals, the scarring of a landscape by open-cast mining, and the ravaging of forests without replanting. As in its traditional sense, poaching is a crime, but the victims are human beings – our current generation and future generations.

Continuing concern about environmental responsibility makes a willingness by companies to show clearly their commitment to creating a better world as essential. Those unable to do so will forfeit the custom of the 'New Customer'.

Social Sensitivity

Social sensitivity is sometimes a bed-fellow of environmental responsibility, but at other times it stands alone. The 'New Customer' will be sensitive to the ways in which companies respond to the needs of three social groups:

- Children.
- The very old.
- The disadvantaged.

Over the next decade there will be an increase in the number of children who live in one parent families, split families and families where both parents go out to work. Children will, therefore, be expected to take care of themselves to a greater extent, and they will, as a result, become customers as well as consumers. Companies will naturally want to benefit from this market and will provide a range of what hitherto had been considered as 'adult products'. This will be so particularly in the food and drinks industries. The temptation to take advantage of children's still forming emotions and appetites will need to be resisted. The 'New Customer' will expect manufacturers and services, such as fast food, entertainment and clothing, to be *in loco parentis*, safeguarding the interests of children, rather than exploiting them. This should not be looked on as idealistic altruism; the Disney organisation has shown that high premiums can be charged and huge profits made by catering for children in a socially sensitive manner.

The fastest growing part of most countries' populations are the 'Very Old' – people who survived to the traditional 'three score years and ten'. People 80 years of age and beyond fall into four broad categories:

1. Self-reliant – living with a partner or by themselves and meeting their own needs.
2. Partially self-reliant – living with a partner or by themselves with help in meeting some of their needs.
3. In care – living in accommodation for the healthy, and assisted in meeting all or most of their needs.
4. Hospitalised – suffering from physical and/or mental disability, and receiving medical supervision.

Each category represents a niche within a niche market. Furthermore, there is what might be called 'shadow markets' for categories two and three – the children of the 'Very Old' who partially or completely take care of their parents. The members of this parental support group are in fact parenting their parents, they are engaged in a role of 'second parenthood'. It is a role for which few, if any, have been prepared.

History has shown how easy it can be to exploit the old and enfeebled. The lure of products which will reverse the ageing process, provide instant wealth or cure painful ailments, have claimed that most pitiful customer – the seeker of the unattainable. No doubt charlatans will continue to take advantage of the 'Very Old', but the growth in their numbers and their accompanying carers will create a 'New Customer' force of increasing power and influence. To cope with this, companies will have to redesign their products and services for the old in a socially sensitive way. Those who fail will incur the wrath not simply of the 'Very Old', but of their descendants, who one day will also be 'Very Old'.

The third 'New Customer' market requiring social sensitivity is the 'disadvantaged', an amorphous group which needs to be sub-divided into:

- Physically and mentally disadvantaged.
- Economically disadvantaged.
- Socially disadvantaged.
- Politically disadvantaged.

Companies which exploit these groups, by making their situation no better or even worse, will find themselves targets for consumer action in the caring 1990s. The triple role of customer/citizen/producer will come into sharper focus; what cannot be attained in the market place will be achieved through the ballot box. It will therefore be in the self-interest of companies to display social sensitivity, not simply by financing 'good causes', but by being willing to help the disadvantaged help themselves through projects, providing employment, and raising self-esteem. The 'New Customer' will expect service providers to show care to all customers regardless of their social status and individual capabilities. Companies will learn that to boost profits you need to boost spirits. This is particularly true of the final cluster of values professed by the 'New Customer'.

Personal fulfilment is the shortest route to delight. Buoyed up by a sense of achievement, enhanced self-worth and self-confidence, the 'New Customer' will seek out those who can help him or her sustain these conditions.

In future there will be two contra-flowing streams of customer behaviour. The 'New Customer' will seek to avoid performing chores and unappealing life maintaining activities. On the other hand, there will be a desire to be more involved in the processing and delivery of life enhancing and life changing activities. As customers become better educated and more consumer aware, they will seek greater control of the services which they are depending upon to solve their problems. Professionalism in the broadest sense will have an important role to play in what might be termed 'shared care'. To save money or speed up the service process, the 'New Customer' will be willing to perform some activities previously undertaken by the service provider. This could involve the completion of documentation, transportation of equipment, self-diagnosis, self-catering, self-check in at airports, or self-checkout at supermarkets. None of these practices are new, what will be new is the automated support systems available to encourage shared care. By feeling more involved in finding solutions to challenging problems, and less involved in what is drudgery, the 'New Customer' will enjoy a greater sense of personal fulfilment, a stronger feeling of delight.

Conclusion

The 'New Customer' brings to each significant purchasing decision an amalgam of values. The greater the congruity between the satisfaction of customer needs with the value system, the more likely the chances of delight. As we move through the 1990s the biblical observation that 'man does not live by bread alone' will be more evident than before. Things of the spirit will play a greater role in shaping our lives as customers/citizens/producers. But benefiting from this shift in values requires new thinking on how best to appeal to the spirit. This is the subject of the next chapter.

Chapter 4

Releasing the Spirit of Customer Care

Introduction

Until the latter half of the nineteenth century the 'customer', in the sense in which we use the word today, did not exist. Most societies were divided into two types of consumer – the patron and the buyer. The rich bestowed their patronage on the providers of luxuries, while the poor could only afford to buy necessities. Freedom of choice for the majority of the poor was severely restricted. In some cases employees could only buy from the 'company' store, and often at exorbitant prices. In all cases, outside of cities, choice was limited to what was available in the local shops.

But as the capacity of industry to produce a variety of products increased, it brought with it scope for greater freedom of choice. A mass market came into being and in its wake came department stores, retail chains, mail order, advertising and other services. To compete in this market it was necessary to rely, not only on price, but on appealing to social status, aesthetics, and self-image. A growth in the size and affluence of the middle classes created a new type of 'customer' seeking more than the bare necessities, but unable to afford exclusive luxuries.

By the dawn of the twentieth century there appeared three phenomena which through the ensuing decades would affect the spirit of customer care:

- Discretionary purchasing power.
- Discretionary time.

- Discretionary behaviour.

Of course, there were other pressures at work, such as the rise of trades unions, wars, and economic cycles. Each of these affected the standard of living and lifestyle of consumers, but here we are concentrating on matters of the spirit rather than economics and social change.

Discretionary Purchasing Power

Throughout most of history, humankind has been pre-occupied with self-preservation. The hours of light were devoted to sowing and reaping, and later to labouring and machine minding; the hours of darkness were spent recuperating from the rigours of day-to-day existence.

The Industrial Revolution led to opportunities to create wealth, the surplus arising from the profits of production and sales. For the few, the industrialists and merchants, the 'surplus' amounted to millions of pounds; for the majority, the 'surplus' would be counted in pennies. This surplus income, regardless of the amount, provided people with choice. For the first time in history there was a substantial number of people who could exercise their right to:

- Purchase non-essentials.
- Postpone gratification to a time of their choosing.
- Substitute one type of expenditure for another.

With the costs of necessities covered, customers can use what remains of their income at their discretion. This enables them to cater for needs of the spirit as well as those of the body, such as food and shelter. Non-essentials could be described as life-enhancing goods and services. Without them life would go on, but would be less pleasurable. The major life enhancing industries, such as entertainment, fashion, restaurants, hotels, and sport have to attract discretionary income to survive. This they do by either changing the perception of the customer to make the non-essential appear essential, or by emphasising the indulgence aspect of their product or service. The first approach might be termed, 'You must have/do this to live the way you want to', while the second approach is usually summed up by, 'Go on, you owe it to yourself'. Both make an appeal to the spirit – in the first case it is striving for a better life; in the second it is reaping the rewards of one's efforts.

Saving provides a mechanism for enjoying the results of striving by being able to postpone gratification and thereby choose a more appealing gratifier than would otherwise have been the case. Whether gratification is instant or postponed, discretionary income enables us to seek delight in a variety of ways. Its main influence on the spirit of customer care is that it provides the economic means by which we can achieve the realisation of our life goals.

Discretionary Time

The growth in affluence in the twentieth century has provided more than discretionary purchasing power, it has extended the period within which that power can be enjoyed. The trade union aspiration of 'eight hours for work, eight hours for sleep, and eight hours for what we will', is a reality in most developed countries. For many, it is the 'eight hours for what we will' that provide the main source of delight. Longer vacation periods, more time spent in retirement, and shorter working hours all provide people with time which they can use at their will. In relation to the spirit of customer care, this 'free time' is the period for self actualisation, enabling individuals to pursue interests which bring pleasure.

All service providers compete for their customers' discretionary time, but there is a group of service providers from whom others can learn – the hedonistic industries. Films, television, sports, vacation, resorts, art galleries, theme parks, publishing – each seeks to appeal to the hedonistic side of us all.

As we shall explore later in this book, the hedonistic industries provide insights into how to awaken and sustain the spirit of customer care. One way (see Chapter 2) is to help people shape their time; another is to help shape their behaviour.

Discretionary Behaviour

In truth, virtually all behaviour is discretionary, but I use the term to highlight a major change affecting behaviour in the twentieth century – the impact of mass education and the media in making people more aware of the options which they have in choosing their behaviour to pursue their goals. Innate abilities have been honed by educational methods which release human potential. Cinema, and subsequently television, have created an awareness of different cultures, different lifestyles, and different approaches to responding to the demands of the human condition. In particular, there has been an urge to enjoy life to the full, not in a sybaritic pursuit of luxury, but as a hedonistic balance compensating for life's travails. People use their discretionary behaviour not only in terms of entertainment, but in acts of charity, self-development, and giving pleasure to others. However, given the choice of behaviour that gives pleasure to the self or which results in self-inflicted pain, the rational person will choose the former.

Pain comes in many forms, from mild irritation to acute suffering – it afflicts both body and the mind. Likewise, pleasure is derived from many sources. Sensual pleasures come from gratifying the needs of the body; aesthetic pleasures from the enjoyment of all things beautiful; and vicarious pleasures reflect our joy in the satisfaction of others. There is a dark side to pleasure – *schadenfreude* – where we revel in the misfortune of others. But on the whole, pleasure enhances rather than diminishes the human spirit. There is therefore advantage in focusing on the hedonistic dimension of any service when we aspire to provide customer care that delights.

Searching for Delight

From time immemorial humankind has sought satisfaction of both spiritual and material needs. For most of the first millennium, spiritual needs were catered for by a major service industry – the church. Art and music all had direct or indirect religious connotations. This synchronicity of service and religion continued well into the second millennium. The separation of church and state was mirrored by the separation of the church and the arts. New art forms, the development of musical instruments, and the invention of printing all contributed to expressions of the human spirit quite separate from the beliefs and practices of religious groups.

The spirit was re-conceptualised as an intangible force which influences the values and beliefs of people and determines the manner in which they are expressed. As the second millennium draws to its end, there are emerging industries which seek to profit from that part of the human spirit which pursues joyful living. There are, of course, many facets of the human spirit other than pleasure: altruism, faith, inspiration, creativity, love and hate are all part of the psyche. Many would claim that, with the exception of hate, they represent nobler aspects than pleasure. So be it, but most of us perceive 'having a good time' as a principal and legitimate pursuit and we search for those who will provide it.

During the twentieth century the development of a mass market for goods has been mirrored by the spread of a mass market for entertainment. This market has six major segments:

1. Arts.
2. Media.
3. Occasions arrangers.
4. Pastimes.
5. Sports.
6. Tourism.

The hedonistic industries have one product – pleasurable experience. They are in the delight business; success depends on continuously delighting their customers. Unfortunately, as with products, tastes change; the delight of yesteryear becomes the bore of today. To remain in business the hedonistic industries need to awaken, appeal to and enlarge the human spirit. While each sets about this in different ways, there is a commonality in the stages which they go through. No matter the industry, each must:

- Arouse interest.
- Engage attention.
- Evoke absorption.
- Transform the experience.
- Transcend the expected.

These stages are fully discussed in Chapter 5. For the moment, a brief comment on the spiritual dimensions will put them in perspective. Arousing interest means awakening the spirit, rousing it from the hidden depths of the psyche, and stimulating it. Film trailers, advertising, providing snatches of music, and listing future magazine contents are all aimed at arousing the interest of the customer. However, care needs to be taken to avoid hype – the over-stimulation of interest. Another danger is that of the unwelcomed intrusion. This happens when time spent on attempting to attract the attention of the customer to a future event detracts from the enjoyment of the current event so that the spirit is stifled at the very time it should be aroused. Feelings of resentment smother feelings of joy.

Engaging attention calls for action which will hold fast the involvement of the customer. If he or she is to be engrossed in the activity, the hedonistic provider must eliminate or reduce all distractions. This requires close attention to the tangible which might destroy the intangible. Sound, lights, lay-out, and decor must all focus on strengthening the psychic bonds which retain the attention of the customer. Once distracted it is difficult to re-engage attention and thus to keep alight the awakened spirit.

Whether stimulated by the goal-scoring skill of a footballer, the melodious harmony of an orchestra, or the colour and perspective of an Old Master, without total absorption there will not be total delight. Evoking absorption results in the state of suspended belief, loss of self-awareness, and a feeling of total commitment to the success of the artist or event which casts a quilt of joy over the bare bones of reality. The stage setting becomes whatever the playwright requires; the printed pages become windows into the soul of the writer; or the splodges of paint become stars in the heaven. The experience transforms the perceptions and feeling of the customer, whether as spectator or participant.

Delightful transforming experiences are the hallmark of successful hedonistic companies. The extent of the transformation may be small, a shift from indifference to amusement, but unless there is some enhancement of the spirit the efforts expended in the earlier stages will be dissipated. Transformation need not be related only to mood; it may be the development of a new skill at sport, a growth of self-awareness, the acquisition of a new taste, new insights into the meaning of a work of art, a sense of identity with an artist, or a feeling of uplift. Whatever its nature, there is only one person who can know the type and extent of the transformation of the spirit – the customer.

The chances of a delightful transforming experience are largely dependent on that experience being better than expected. Transcending the expected is not easy. It manifests itself in the pleasant surprise. To be effective the surprise need not be great – the vital elements are timing and feelings. The more unexpected, the greater the surprise, and the more positive the feelings it evokes in both the surprised person and others privy to the secret, the more beneficial its effect on their spirits. From the 'surprise endings' of films and novels to the unexpected wonders of Disneyland, customers seek experiences which give a joyful fillip to their lives, not a sudden jolt.

Transplanting the Hedonistic Features

Transplanting human organs is a risky business, but the main risk lies less in the actual operation than in the eventual rejection of the transplanted organ by the recipient's immune system. So too, with transferring customer care practices from one industry to another. Each industry has its own 'immune system' in terms of traditions, customer relationships and other characteristics, which can make it difficult for new approaches to take hold. This is particularly true in relation to features of hedonistic industries transferred to other types of services.

There are two ways by which the process of assimilation of the 'new' can be made easier for a company. The first is to determine the type of customer care they provide, then to consider themselves as an 'hedonistic company' rather than a 'service company', and develop the pleasure dimension of their distinctive type of care.

Banks, for example, are primarily in the wealth-care business, medical services in health care, hairdressing in beauty care, and airlines in travel-time care. By thinking of the function of service industries in this way, it becomes apparent that to provide the appropriate care it is necessary to involve the customer in the process:

- Airline passengers must check in for their flight at the appropriate time if they are to fly.

- Bank customers must keep to their part of a financial deal if the bank is to help them prosper.

- Patients need to describe their ailments and follow the regime prescribed for them if they are to be restored to health.

- Hairdressers have to know how an individual wants to look in order to contribute to the desired self-image.

The more the customer is involved in the caring process, the more likely he or she will be satisfied with the outcome. Their expectations will be set at a more realistic level by gaining insights into the feasibility of solving their problems within the constraints imposed on the service provider. Their fresh eye may well spot opportunities to enhance the process; a bond of mutual respect will be forged if both customer and provider are willing to give of their best in problem-solving. A true sense of 'shared care' will delight both parties.

However, customer involvement must be given willingly and only sought when it is necessary in order to provide the solution desired by the customer, and where it is likely to make the customer feel good or shape time in the way the customer wants.

This structured interplay between provider and customer will, at its best, create a service symbiosis in which each recognises and respects their inter-dependency. The concept of symbiosis is important to releasing the spirit of care since it helps both provider and customer to focus on the process from a new perspective. In place of the traditional concept of the customer as a passive recipient of service, it highlights that customers play a key role in determining the quality of care which they receive. From the viewpoint of the 'service provider', the concept changes the customer from recipient to partner. No customer can be delighted against his or her will; only when all the conditions are right will the customer open the psychic gate to the spirit of delight. Service symbiosis is one of the keys which will unlock the hedonistic gate.

All service industries have a hedonistic, or pleasure-giving dimension; it varies in size depending on personality and circumstances. However, in broad terms, the opportunity of the provider to create a sense of delight will depend on the type of problem which the customer is seeking to resolve. As mentioned in Chapter 2, the problems dealt with by service industries fall into three categories:

- Life maintaining.
- Life enhancing.
- Life changing.

Enabling the customer to resolve life maintaining problems will result in 'good feelings', usually of low intensity and short duration. Success by dry cleaners in removing a stain, having a well-cooked hamburger swiftly served or undertaking a comfortable and punctual train journey, can all be pleasurable experiences, but they are unlikely to cause unbounded rejoicing. Providers of day-to-day or *quotidian* services should recognise this reality and not set too ambitious delight goals.

Satisfying life enhancing needs provides more opportunities to exploit the hedonistic dimension. We have already seen that a number of industries are in the business of life enhancement. Delight associated with their success in meeting the customers' needs is therefore likely to be more intense, and of longer duration, than is the case with life maintenance. A problem for life enhancers is that customers come to them with an expectation of being delighted. A hedonistic threshold has been established in the mind of the customer; if the provider stumbles over it the chances of delighting the customer will be dashed and lost.

Life changing needs will not always be capable of being resolved in a manner that delights; death is rarely a hedonistic experience, nor is coping with a failed marriage or business. Nevertheless, where potential for the hedonistic factor exists, those who provide solutions to life changing problems are in a position to release feelings of intense joy whose effects are experienced over long time-spans.

How best then to translate the features of hedonistic industries to other services which have a more limited scope for providing pleasures? The best approach is to broaden the perspectives of the service provider.

Widening the Perspectives

The two ways in which the perspectives of those engaged in providing services can be widened are role exchange and context exchange.

Role exchange is relatively common; role plays in which service providers play the parts of 'customers' have long been used in customer care training. This role play approach is sometimes carried further by having employees experience what it is like to be a customer by putting them through a 'real life' experience, by seeking service in parts of the company in which they are unknown. Another type of exchange is to have employees visit competitors in the role of customers.

Each approach has its merits, but in terms of managing the Delight Factor, role exchange has limited value. This is due to the fact that delight is a function of expectations. No matter how hard the role players try, their expectations are unlikely to be exceeded since they are more familiar with the context in which they are performing their customer role than an actual customer would be. Therefore, to widen perspectives it is better to bring about a change of context than a change of roles.

There are three ways by which context can be changed:

- Metaphor.
- Geography.
- Design.

Delight through a Metaphor

The use of a metaphor requires a service provider to identify a hedonistic industry as a counterpart from which it can adopt and adapt ways of managing the Delight Factor. Having identified the appropriate counterpart, the next step is to seek out the similarities in the way each company serves its customers, and where there is scope for the service company to learn from the hedonistic company.

Providers of the mundane, such as banks, post offices, and supermarkets, can imagine themselves to be in one or more of the hedonistic industries and identify elements which could be adopted to make the mundane more pleasurable. The theatre provides lessons for all seeking to manage the Delight Factor. A successful performance of, say, an opera is marked by the following characteristics:

- A synthesis of story, music, acting and decor, providing the customer with a holistic, rather than a fragmented hedonistic experience.
- Though sharing the experience with others, the performance is interpreted on a personal basis depending on the extent to which the individual is 'educated' on all aspects of opera. The better the understanding, the greater the likelihood of enjoyment.
- The success of the performance is dependent on all the performers being fully rehearsed and interpreting their roles in a manner which they believe will provide the customer with pleasure.
- During the performance all props are available on cue; all hand-overs are made smoothly and on time.
- Regardless of the length of the run, each performance is fresh; the commitment and enthusiasm of the performers retains the glow of the first night.
- Although the principals have leading roles, there is an ensemble approach to the acting and singing.
- Back stage staff play their roles out of sight of the customers, but are aware of their important contribution to the success of every performance.
- The response of the audience, if positive, will provide the oxygen of appreciation which will move the performers to give more than they may have thought possible. If negative, both performers and customers will suffer from a lack of pleasure.

One of the world's most successful hedonistic companies, Disney, has long practised the use of a metaphor at its Disney World pleasure parks. All employees are trained to think and perform as though they were on stage; they are referred to as 'cast members' and are expected to follow 'scripts' in ways that will enhance the Delight Factor. Of course, it can be argued that people only visit Disney World because they seek pleasure, and so it is relatively easy to pander to their needs. However, other pleasure park companies have tried to emulate the Disney approach, using the designation 'cast' to describe their employees. Many of these copy-cats have failed since they have not recognised that Disney prospers by instilling a spirit of delight-giving by its staff, decor, and layout. This requires more than a change of labels; it needs careful selection, training and motivating of people so that they want to give delight.

Even Disney can have problems in providing the Delight Factor. Despite its success in transferring its theme park to Tokyo, it faced problems in 1992 when making a similar transfer to Paris. In planning Euro-Disney, the American executives focused only on the second part of the hyphenated title. While the contrast between sunny Florida and rain-swept France was taken into account, less obvious but important cultural characteristics were ignored. In particular, the insistence on no consumption of one's own food and drink resulted in what almost amounted to body searches at the point of entry. The failure to provide convenient parking for coaches (a more common mode of transport to events in Europe than in America) caused long walks before reaching the entrance.

Added to these physical and psychological irritants, there were at least two 'spiritual' concerns: a belief that staff were being exploited, and a perception of an American cultural invasion. All these factors built a wall of resentment in the minds of customers which required Herculean efforts to break down and allow delight to enter. The lesson for Disney, as for all others who seek to provide delight, is to avoid the assumption that what delights one customer segment will delight others.

Nevertheless, there is much to learn from Disney which can benefit other industries. Fast food chains are not a hedonistic industry, basically they are providers of the mundane – standardised portions of standardised foods. However,

McDonalds, Burger King and the like have differentiated themselves more by the Delight Factor than by the quality of their food. They are outstanding examples of the use of a metaphor to widen the perspectives of their staff and customers – from being food providers to being food pleasure providers.

Airlines have long been aware that they need to provide entertainment on long journeys. Every day, aircraft cabins across the globe are transformed into cinemas, often more comfortable and efficient than the 'real' cinema. This is part of the metaphor of 'airlines as entertainment'. The provision of personal video screens on aircraft is a recent additional playing out of the metaphor. As more people fly, and therefore there are more first-time flyers, airlines will provide increasing ways of keeping customers entertained. This will be particularly true of trips to holiday resorts, since by definition vacationers are 'pleasure seekers'. The holiday will begin from check in.

Banks are not places where people go in search of pleasure. Fear, dread, anxiety, and boredom are the feelings which many customers experience in their contact with banks. Money is a serious business. Attempts to transform banking halls into fun palaces are doomed to failure. Nevertheless, banks can gain benefit from a metaphor in terms of another service industry whose customers experience fear, dread and anxiety – medical services. This metaphor has been used to a limited extent in such phrases as:

- 'There is a healthy credit balance'.
- 'We're putting this company in intensive care'.
- 'We'll need to apply drastic surgery'.
- 'Financial advice clinic'.

However, extending the metaphor, bank branches might look on themselves as medical centres and their customers as patients with real and imagined ailments, many of them psychological rather than physical. Reassurance, hope, and professional behaviour are as important to bank customers as details of financial cures for their economic ills. The customers need to be made aware that unless they give full and true details of their condition, there is a danger of the wrong medicine being prescribed and their situation being worsened. Preventative action rather than post-crisis cures is a principle as important in banking as in medical services.

If bank managers considered their role to be akin to doctors, they might be more willing to leave their offices and visit their 'patients' on site. This brings us to the second device for encouraging new perspectives – geography.

Delight through Geography

Providing familiar services in unfamiliar surroundings can make them more pleasurable, if the location is attractive. Hair dressing salons on cruise liners are an example of making a chore more pleasurable. The success of Tupperware shows how a product as mundane as a plastic container can be sold by making the point-of-sale a party-type occasion.

Relocation of services can increase the Delight Factor by making their availability more convenient for the customer. Car servicing workshops at railway stations are an example. Their proximity to another form of transport removes the need for the customer to arrange alternative transport to and from the service centre.

Likewise, more services, such as cash dispensers and vending machines, are becoming available on-site at hospitals, universities and other densely populated service delivery points. Home shopping by television is perhaps the most outstanding example of relocating service. Although some might claim that it indulges the lazy, it will be a great boon to those who through no fault of their own are house-bound or isolated from shopping centres.

Delight through Design

Design is the third leg of the tripod of perspective changes. It can be used in relation to the Delight Factor in three ways:

- To enlarge the hedonistic dimension.
- To counteract negative perceptions.
- To give substance to the intangible.

The design of premises, both internally and externally, can make a significant contribution to the Delight Factor. We are all affected by our surroundings. Colour, texture, and smell make an impact on emotions and senses. We are disturbed by incongruities. Gas light-fittings in the cabin of an aircraft would arouse anxiety rather than admiration; similarly, neon-lit advertising on the walls of a medieval castle is more likely to repel than attract custom.

The purpose of corporate design is to create a corporate identity which results in a positive image in the eyes of the customer. From logo to stationery there should be a symmetry of identifying features which the customer associates with the company concerned, and which differentiates it from its rivals. Design can enlarge the hedonistic dimension in many ways, including:

- Conveying an appearance which is welcoming, warm and displays a sense of fun.
- Providing customer areas which are comfortable and relaxing.
- Creating an ambience which makes transactions for the customer more pleasurable than expected.
- Enabling staff to join in the festive spirit in a manner which is wholly acceptable to the customer.

Obviously 'design for fun' is a long-established practice in hedonistic industries. The opulence of theatres and cinemas is an example of adding to the pleasure of customers by enabling them to experience a higher level of luxury than they could afford in their home surroundings. Las Vegas with its extraordinary hotels and casinos is an extreme example of the use of design to enlarge the hedonistic dimensions of the services which the city provides.

Less startling, but no less effective, is the interior design of department stores such as Harrods with its Egyptian Hall, where the wonders of ages past are transported through time to boost sales in the present.

Design can also be effective in counteracting the negative perceptions of customers. Banks have spent fortunes in making their previously austere premises 'customer friendly'. The cabins of aircraft use interior design to hide electrical and mechanical systems, and reduce the anxiety of passengers by using colours which are soothing. Airports, which are in effect giant waiting rooms, counteract negative feelings associated with waiting, by providing attractive, comfortable lounges and diversions such as 'play areas' for children.

Finally, design can be used to give substance to the intangible. Insurance policies, mortgages, loans, and investment accounts are intangibles. Well-designed documents can give them substance. On a larger scale, buildings can be used to convey a sense of stability, modernity, dependability and other intangible values.

Conclusion

Releasing the spirit of customer care requires in-depth knowledge of your customers' needs, wants and desires. Service providers have to tap into the discretionary purchasing power, time and behaviour of those they seek to serve. Hedonistic industries such as cinema, theatre, and sport provide models which less pleasure-oriented services can adopt. The use of a metaphor, geography and design will encourage those who provide customer care with greater opportunities to release its spirit for the benefit of themselves and the customer. There is a five-step approach in managing the Delight Factor which can be adapted for any service:

1. Arouse interest.
2. Engage attention.

3. Evoke absorption.
4. Transform the experience.
5. Transcend the expected.

In the next chapter this approach is covered in detail.

Chapter 5
The Delight Makers

Introduction

The fastest growing industries in the world are devoted to mass entertainment, relaxation and enlightenment. These hedonistic industries are the purveyors of life pleasures; they seek to satisfy humankind's need to escape from the mundane. There are three other avenues of escape: self-fulfilment, love of others, and religion. What distinguishes the hedonistic industries is that they provide pleasure for money. In return for payment, the delight-makers provide three types of pleasure products and services:

- Life exploiting.
- Life diverting.
- Life enhancing.

By studying the ways in which the purveyors of pleasure win and keep their audiences we can discover clues on how to manage delight in more mundane industries.

Purveyors of Pleasure

'Life Exploiters' are engaged in providing products and services which take advantage of human frailty and ignorance. Often operating outside the law, they pander to our baser emotions and distorted senses. Brothels, gambling, and drug abuse are at one end of the spectrum; less dramatic, but nevertheless exploitative, are 'cheap and nasty' products – kitsch

– and 'cheap and nasty' thrills, ranging from strip-tease to video nasties. The life exploiters debase human nature, and provide warnings rather than models for those who seek to manage the Delight Factor. *Schadenfreude* – taking malicious delight in the misfortune of others – is the antithesis of customer care; life exploiters care only for themselves. Their activities leave in their wake despair rather than delight.

'Life Diverters' are in the entertainment business, providing legitimate diversion from the demands of everyday life. Their aim is to amuse, relax or stimulate their customers in ways that are unharmful, undemanding, yet embellish life by giving people a 'good time'. The manner in which they offer experiences that delight provides useful models for those striving to produce the same effect in more mundane industries. 'Life Diverters' ask little of their customers apart from enjoying themselves and paying for the privilege. Whereas access to the 'Life Exploiters' is through the spy-hole doors, it is the open turnstile and box office which provide entry to diversions such as sports events, cinemas and theatres.

'Life Enhancers' provide more than diversion: they are sources of inspiration, enlightenment and personal development, both mentally and physically. They give pleasure in ways that add to the quality of life, enabling their customers to acquire knowledge and skills, experience emotions and exercise the senses in both traditional and new patterns of delight. The visual arts, music, literature, and participative sports enable those who wish to move to higher planes of self-actualisation at play and at work. They provide useful models on how best to manage the Delight Factor.

All three types of hedonistic products and services – exploitative, diverting and enhancing – are to be found in each of the six major categories of delight makers:

- Arts.
- Media.
- Arrangers of occasions.

- Pastimes.
- Sports.
- Tourism.

Regardless of the category, the delight-maker has to take account of:

- The types of hedonistic experience its customers want.
- The contribution required of the customer to bring about the experience.
- The frequency of the experience.
- The duration of the experience.
- The location of the experience.

Types of Hedonistic Experience

For reasons previously stated, we shall ignore the experiences offered by exploitative companies, concentrating on those delight-makers whose products and services are diverting or enhancing.

Customers desire from 'Life Diverting' companies experiences which provide delight by banishing, however temporarily, their day-to-day worries and preoccupations. Throughout the period of the experience, the delight-makers strive to provide diversions which evoke emotions in a low-key way, stimulating and then satisfying the senses. A feeling of contentment should continue after the cessation of the diversion. Like the act of love, all other hedonistic experiences have three phases: stimulation of mind and body, consummation of desire, and after-glow of shared contentment. Just as in the act of love, absence of the stimulation and post-coital contentment debases the experience at best to a mechanical coupling, at worst to rape; so too will a diverting or enhancing hedonistic experience be rendered less pleasurable if the Delight Factor is missing at any stage in the encounter between pleasure provider and customer.

'Life Enhancers' are providers of the more noble forms of pleasure. Their efforts aim to enthral the emotions, enlighten the mind and exhilarate the senses. While 'Life Diverters' strive to give their customers a 'good time out', the enhancer's role is to help people 'get out of themselves'. 'Life Enhancers' provide hedonistic experiences which can be transforming as well as enhancing. The materialistic tycoon loses himself in opera; the harried teacher is renewed by visiting an art gallery; or the hard-headed politician sheds a tear as she finishes a novel.

As previously stated, both diverters and enhancers must follow a five-stage process if they are to succeed:

- Arouse interest.
- Engage attention.
- Evoke absorption.
- Transform the experience.
- Transcend the expected.

At each stage there is the involvement of emotions and/or the senses. The mix and intensity of their involvement in the pleasure process will vary between individuals, and at different phases in our personal development. As we age we change our preferences for being entertained, and our capacity for finding delight in certain forms of entertainment is reduced. The reasons will range from impairment of the senses, particularly sight and hearing, to the loss of a sense of mystery. Once we know how the trick works it no longer delights.

However, throughout our lives there are competing opportunities to be entertained, and therefore the first task of the purveyor of entertainment is to capture our interest, and to alert us to the possibility of finding delight in one pursuit in preference to another. The circus announces its arrival with garish bill-posters, the film-maker publicises the favourable endorsement of a respected critic, or the star of the new play appears on radio and television chat shows.

This arousal stage soon slides into growing or lessening interest. Excerpts of films, plays, or television programmes lay down a trail of things to come which build up a framework of expectations. Should it prove a false trail we will feel cheated and bereft of the anticipated delights. Managing expectations is a critical aspect of delight-making. Set too high they will result in disappointment; too low and they discourage us from pursuing the entertainment on offer.

Today many forms of entertainment fall victim to exaggerated claims or hype for their delight potential. In effect, the Delight Factor is smothered beneath the rubble of broken promises and smashed expectations. It is a fundamental truth of delight-making that unless expectations are exceeded, the customer will not experience delight.

The 'engaging attention' stage is the outcome of having our interest aroused. Engagement can range in intensity from total absorption to surface presence. Total absorption is marked by a suspension of those factors which might otherwise impede intense enjoyment. There is complete acceptance of the scene being witnessed, the passage being read, or the music being heard. No other world exists but that which the customer is experiencing at that point in time.

Surface presence, on the other hand, is minimal engagement. Although physically present, the mind of the customer is elsewhere. There is a lack of interest in the pleasure being provided, an awareness of every distraction, and a tendency to react to the entertainment as individual entities, scenery, costumes, and script, rather than to enjoy it as an integrated whole.

Without attention phasing into absorption it will not be possible to experience the next phase – transformation. This is a satiation of needs, an exceeding of expectations, a metamorphosis from viewer or listener into a full participant in the experience shared with the performers. Fulfilment through transformation is the peak of the delight experience. It may last minutes or hours, but there needs to be a move down from the summit, not a tumble, but a measured and comfortable descent.

As a consequence of success at the transformation stage, the customer will have had his or her expectations exceeded. Glowing from this transcendence, the customer experiences pleasure and the delight-maker experiences success.

Delight Devices

Delight-makers use a range of sensual and emotional devices to ensure the pleasure of their patrons. These range from imagination-capturing to emotional arousal, from nostalgia to surprise. The choice being determined by that part of the psyche which the delight provider seeks to affect.

Capturing the imagination can be achieved in many ways, including:

- Leaving the listener to set the scene for a radio play.
- Producing special effects which provide fantasy worlds that appear real.
- Using tricks of the camera to create impressions of having witnessed events which did not take place.
- Using sounds to evoke images in the mind of the listener.
- Making the 'impossible' appear to happen.

Arousing emotion has always been part of the delight-makers' art. Whether by fear of the unknown, sympathy for victims, detestation of villains, or joy at the triumph of heroes and heroines, dramatists, authors and film-makers set out to play on the heart strings of their audience. In these circumstances, delight can be the result of the interplay of positive feelings or the elimination of negative ones. The latter is to be found in those situations where feelings of fear or anxiety are aroused but then removed when the dreaded event does not take place.

The process of catharsis whereby there is a purging of the emotions through the impact of drama has its roots in the theatre of ancient Greece. In fact many of the devices used on stage and screen have been passed down through the centuries. Each category of delight-maker uses the devices in different ways, but in each case the five-stage pleasure process comes into play (in all senses of the word). The following summary focuses on how different categories of delight-makers operate; it is not intended to be an in-depth analysis of the total operations of each industry.

The Arts

The arts can be classified in various ways: visual, performing, decorative, liberal, and literary. The common thread is that they are manifestations of the creative capabilities of humankind. They provide ways which affirm the ability of the human spirit to transcend the mundane and the demeaning; they arouse positive feelings, stretch the imagination, and conjure up deeper insights and wider perspectives in both the artist and beholder. The specific ways in which this is brought about will depend on the particular art form.

Music

Music stirs the mind and can stimulate the vocal chords and the limbs, depending on its harmonic construction and intent. The pervasiveness of music in our daily life, particularly the use of muzak in offices, shops and airports, can deafen us to the Delight Factor in musical composition. Down the ages composers have been sensitive to the different ways of evoking delight, creating moods, diverting and entrancing us at different times; aubades were originally compositions to be performed in the morning, nocturnes in the evening. From berceuse, or cradle song, to requiem, there is music appropriate to all of life's stages.

The five-stage process for managing the Delight Factor is reflected in different types of musical composition. A major work may contain some of the following elements:

- Prelude, to arouse interest.
- Fugue, to engage attention by using several themes which are first stated separately, then developed in counterpoint.
- Reprise, to evoke absorption by the repetition of a phrase, or return to an earlier theme.
- Crescendo or diminuendo, to transform the experience from one of listening to one of being transported by sound.
- Coda, to transcend the expected by introducing a short additional passage at the end of the composition.

There are, of course, other ways in which the blending of melody and rhythm can complete the delight process. Whatever the approach, music reminds us that delight is no accident, but requires careful composition in terms of notes and tempo; the blending of complementary themes; and teamwork if it is not a solo piece – mastery of the tools of the trade, so to speak. The dividing line between the pleasure of music and the pain of cacophony is a thin one; once crossed the Delight Factor disappears. Opera is an outstanding example of hedonistic overlay, pleasing to the eye as well as the ear. This increases the impact of the Delight Factor. To the melodious skills of the composer are added the writing skills of the dramatist and the scenic skills of the designer. Yet all must blend if there is to be delight rather than disappointment.

Drama

Having described the five-stage process in relation to a musical work, we can now consider it in terms of the drama. Once again we find in classical works devices for each stage:

- Interest is aroused by the use of a prologue which introduces the action of the play. (In the modern theatre this function may be carried out by programme notes.)

- Attention is engaged by the use of 'business', incidental actions by the performers or by *coup de theatre*, whereby there is a sudden turn of events or an astonishing piece of stage craft.

- Absorption of the audience is evoked by such means as *peripeteia*, a twist in the plot or dramatic irony whereby the meaning of the words are understood by the audience but not the characters.

- The experience of the audience may be transformed by such devices as *anagnorisis*, the moment of recognition of the truth by the hero, leading to the denouement or by catharsis which figuratively speaking cleanses the emotions of the audience.

- Expectations will be transcended if the previous four stages have had the desired effect on the audience. The number of curtain calls is a good measure of transcended expectations.

Painting

The third component of opera and drama – scenic design – brings us to the world of painting. As with all other hedonistic occupations, painters can be classified as exploiters, diverters or enhancers. The trouble is that with the passage of time each contemporary viewer may have a classification different from his or her ancestors. Painters spurned in one century become the geniuses of another; painters idolised by previous generations are consigned to the attic by later ones, only to be 'rediscovered' yet again.

This is not the place for an in-depth study of painting – our purpose is to identify the reasons why some works give more delight than others. In many cases, a painting may be little more than a wall covering. Other paintings may evoke negative feelings of disgust or fear; yet others may arouse interest or startle, but their impact is short lived. All of these we will consign to the attic of forgetfulness.

A painting which meets the criteria for giving delight is one which makes demands on the mind as well as the eye:

- Interest is aroused by the combination of colour, light, shade and texture which attracts the eye. What we first see is an arrangement of different colours which register on the retina.

- Our attention is engaged if the meaning of the composition attracts or intrigues us. The artist may communicate by his composition an image which is easy to understand. Whether it is a landscape, portrait, or still life, it is a representation of the tangible. Alternatively, the artist may be seeking to represent the intangible in a work which is abstract. This imposes greater demands on both artist and viewer. At this stage, the artist succeeds in drawing the viewer into his world or loses the viewer altogether.

The extent to which the viewer becomes absorbed in a particular painting will depend on a combination of factors:

- Subject matter.
- Knowledge of the artist's intentions.
- How well the eye of the beholder is trained.
- Emotional and sensory impact.
- Where and how the painting is displayed.

It is an irony of our time that most of the greatest works of art can be viewed only in the busiest art galleries. However, a test of the merits of any painting is its ability to stir the viewer. The true artist transforms the experience of visiting a picture gallery to one of self-renewal by revealing to the viewer a new insight, a widening perspective, an increased self-awareness each time the painting is seen. Expectations are transcended when the phrase, 'I don't know about art, but I know what I like', is replaced by, 'I'm getting to know about art and am continuously surprised by what I like'.

Literature

Literature, like music and painting, has been a major source of delight down the centuries. The written word is not always used to evoke delight, but in terms of being part of a hedonistic industry, books fall into three categories: pornography, escapism, and enlightenment. As with paintings, these categories get redefined over time. Many works we consider to be enlightening were once condemned as pornographic or escapist. Some writers have had the ability to produce books in all three categories; sometimes writers are remembered for only one or two of many works. As with other branches of the arts, success depends on the author's ability to motivate readers to experience delight by going through the five-stage process.

Novelists bring to their work either a Platonic (spiritual or theoretical) tendency, an Aristotelian one (materialistic or empirical), or a combination of the two. These tendencies are blended with national characteristics and historical perspectives which the writer draws upon to create a piece of literature which will move, shock, disturb or delight the reader.

The first stage in the delight process, arousing interest, is critical in literature. If you do not start a book you will never finish it – a trite statement, but one which all writers must keep in mind in devising the opening sentences of novels. Having aroused the reader's interest, the unfolding of the plot, the build-up of the characters and description of events should then engage the attention and have the reader fully absorbed in the fate of the characters. The skilled writer enables the reader to empathise with the situation of the characters and experience their hopes and fears. This transforms the experience from the mere reading of a book to one of living another life. Expectations will be transcended either by the denouement of the story, or by the sense of uplift which the reader experiences as the book is closed. This process applies as much to escapist pot-boilers as to works of literature.

Sculpture, ballet and the cinema are segments of the arts industry. They are not discussed in detail here since the ways in which they manage the Delight Factor are an adaptation of the approaches previously described for painting (sculpture), opera (ballet) and the theatre (cinema).

The Media

The function of newspapers, magazines, radio and television is as much to inform as to entertain. However, even their informing function must be carried out in an entertaining way if it is to gain and retain audience attention. Therefore, they are to some degree a hedonistic industry.

There are four lessons which companies keen to enlarge the hedonistic dimension of their service can learn from the media:

- Reliability and accuracy of service delivery.
- Importance of attention spans.
- Style is as important as content.
- The segmentation of delight seekers.

Daily papers have to be available daily; hourly newscasts have to be delivered on the hour; and a TV programme scheduled to last 60 minutes needs to take up that amount of time – no more, no less. An unexpected blank TV screen or radio silence lasting less than a minute seems much longer to the viewer or listener and has to be explained or apologised for. Communicating concern and apologising for a break in service, however short lived, is something which other service industries can learn from the electronic media.

The second lesson is that customers vary in their attention spans; for many it may be only a minute or so before their minds jump to another subject. The flipping of pages and switching of channels are hazards faced by all engaged in the media. In the process of managing the Delight Factor the media are often brilliant at arousing interest; eye-catching headlines, action-packed trailers, and titillating photographs abound. What distinguishes the best from the not so good is the ability to follow through by engaging attention, evoking absorption, and making the viewer, listener or reader feel that the experience was worthwhile and has exceeded his or her expectations. Over- or under-estimating the attention span of customers greatly reduces the chances of the Delight Factor casting a glow on the experience.

The third lesson which the media provide for managing the Delight Factor is that style can be as important as content. The claim by Marshall McLuan the 'the medium is the message' is manifested day-in and day-out in the newspapers, magazines, television and radio. The same stories are conveyed in different ways to delight different readerships and audiences. New angles, exclusive coverage, and inside information are among the devices used to gain higher ratings or sell more copies. It is the way in which news, views and entertainment are delivered which provides competitive advantage. The media market is highly segmented; newspapers and television programmes are exploitative, diverting or enhancing. Rarely is the reader taken by surprise as to the category into which a newspaper or magazine slots, the front page usually tells it all. This brings us to the fourth lesson – segmentation of the market.

Readers, viewers and listeners rarely flit from one extreme to another in seeking delight. It is rare for readers of scandal sheets to also be devotees of the 'quality press'. Lovers of broadly drawn situation comedy are unlikely to be equally satisfied by political debates. The competitor of *The Times* is not the *Daily Mirror*, but one of the other broad sheet papers. The lesson for those outside the media is that in managing the Delight Factor it is necessary to be better than the customer's perception of who is your rival, not your own perception.

Arrangers of Occasions

This is a clumsy, but descriptive label for one of the fastest growing categories of delight-makers – those who help others to celebrate significant occasions, ranging from birthday parties and weddings to anniversaries of historic events. Their services can range from gift-wrapping to providing a banquet; whatever it is, their aim is to delight.

There are six aspects of managing the Delight Factor which relate to the work of arrangers:

- Context transforms experience
- The ephemeral can be managed.
- What delights people is what delights people.
- Detail dominates delight.
- Little extras can be more efficacious than big surprises.
- Obtrusiveness can kill delight.

Occasions are usually associated with changes in the life of an individual or the history of a nation. Weddings, birthdays, and graduation ceremonies are all causes for individual celebration. National days, religious festivals, and commemoration of revolutions or ends of wars are celebrated across countries and borders. Whatever the celebration, it must provide a context which transforms day-to-day experience. A wedding cake is more than a source of nourishment, and a bride's bouquet is not simply a bunch of flowers; the loyal toast is more than an excuse for an extra drink, just as a honeymoon is more than a holiday.

Arrangers of occasions are sensitive to the changes which context imposes on experience; their role is to guide the celebrants on matters of protocol, to ensure that the transforming experience is not shattered by maladroitness on the part of those involved. In essence their job is to make a special occasion *feel* special. The source of delight can be in observing ritual, as much as in the surprise of the new. When we sense that something is out of context we may be disturbed rather than delighted.

Possessing and communicating a 'sense of occasion' greatly improves the chances for delight.

Providing the sense of occasion is preserved, a change of location from the norm can heighten the delight experience. Hence arrangers of occasions are increasingly offering exotic locations in which to hold a celebration, including museums, aircraft, and zoos. This is likely to grow as traditional constraints on such matters as the location for marriage ceremonies disappear. However, as shown by tragedies such as the sinking of a disco boat in the Thames in 1989 resulting in many of the revellers drowning, the search for the exotic does not always lead to delight.

Occasions by definition are short-lived, rarely lasting more than a day. This ephemeral quality makes it necessary to extend the duration of opportunities to delight by thinking of the ephemeral as having three phases:

- Preparation.
- Realisation.
- Reflection.

Arrangers can make the preparation phase enjoyable by taking on those facets of preparation which their clients find irksome, leaving them to concentrate on what gives them joy. Similarly, at the time of the actual event the arranger can heighten the Delight Factor by carrying out the mundane tasks and clearing the aftermath. The reflection phase follows on as the celebrants look back on the event with feelings of nostalgia, reliving their delight. Arrangers of occasions help here by providing for photographs, film and mementoes of the event which imprint the ephemeral on the mind, thus extending the life-span of the occasion.

The memories of delight we carry in our heads vary widely among individuals. The variation is due to circumstances, personalities, age, intelligence and a host of other factors. Arrangers survive because they know that what delights people is what delights people; nevertheless there can be no guarantee that what is a source of delight to one person will be equally well received by another. Sensitivity to idiosyncrasies is a prerequisite for managing the Delight Factor. In many situations the differentiating factor may be a matter of detail.

Details dominate delight; the tyranny of the trivial haunts arrangers of occasions, and well it might since failure to care for detail can sound the death-knell of delight. Something as simple as too much sugar can transform 'the cup that cheers' into what tastes like poison. The Delight Factor can be destroyed as much by the pinpricks of overlooked detail as by the steam roller of gross incompetence. Arrangers analyse situations down to the last detail; they know that no matter how attractive the picture on a jigsaw is, it takes only one absent piece to spoil it.

Little extras can be more efficacious than big surprises when managing the Delight Factor. Small surprises stimulate the heart; large surprises can stop it. Arrangers use three devices to evoke delight:

- Traditional symbols.
- Personalised tokens.
- Unexpected benefits.

Traditional symbols, often food and drink, are associated with celebrations. The skill of the arranger is to enable the client to comply with tradition, but in a novel fashion. For example, by judicious use of colouring, the champagne used to toast the bridal couple could match the colour scheme chosen by the bride.

Personalised tokens such as books of matches, pencils, or boxes of chocolates imprinted with the name of the guest are not new ideas, but still make a big impression. Most people enjoy seeing their name in print: it is an affirmation of their identity and a boost to their self-esteem. For very little cost an ordinary bottle of wine can be transformed into a source of delight by replacing the standard label with a personalised one.

Unexpected benefits are another way of getting the Delight Factor to work for you. It may be that there is in the order of service booklet at a wedding a pouch into which you can fit the official photograph, which is given to each guest on leaving the reception. Alternatively, the arranger who organised the wedding will send the bridal couple a bottle of wine on their first anniversary. 'Planned spontaneity' may sound like a contradiction in terms, but it is a key technique for managing the Delight Factor.

The final lesson we can learn from the work of arrangers is the need to balance essential presence against obtrusiveness. The less visible the mechanisms of delight are, the greater the level of enjoyment will be. So too with the purveyors of delight. The overbearing master of ceremonies, the noisy waiter, or the lingering porter all diminish the Delight Factor. Knowing when to withdraw in a graceful manner is the mark of the loyal courtier and the skilled arranger of occasions, but in both cases they must also be readily on hand when needed.

Pastimes

All hedonistic activities are in a sense 'pastimes'. The word is used here in a more restricted manner to describe recreational activities which do not fall into one of the other entertainment categories, and which share one or more of the following characteristics:

- Undertaken voluntarily purely for pleasure.
- Individually centred – the 'player' directly contributes to the activity.
- Self-paced – the player (and, where appropriate, fellow participants) determines the start, duration and end of the activity.
- The player directly determines the level of delight.

Pastimes are almost as varied as types of people; they range from gardening to knitting, and from ballroom dancing to yoga.

In most cases individuals indulge in a number of pastimes, depending on age, the seasons, and psychological and physiological needs. The 'pastimes' industry; is diverse, but the common thread running through it is the provision of guidance, equipment and premises which will increase the delight which the individual derives from the pastime or hobby.

The main lessons to be obtained from these hedonistic industries are:

- Context changes behaviour. The shy typist dons her ballgown and dances the tango with abandon; the autocratic boss shouts at subordinates in the office and whispers to flowers in the garden.

- Individuals have hidden depths. The clumsy porter makes meticulously accurate models of ships; the curt colleague becomes the loquacious reciter of his own poems.

- Attention spans vary not simply between people, but from one situation to another. Individuals can devote hours to completing a crossword, but soon tire of completing a jigsaw.

- People compete with themselves as well as with others. Many individuals seek goods and services which will improve their performance in entirely non-competitive activities such as needlework, keeping fit and DIY.

Every customer is multi-faceted, with some parts reflecting more than others. Just as the jeweller needs an eye-piece to assess fully all facets of a gem, so too does the provider of goods and services need to take a close view of a customer to identify opportunities to delight. Those involved in providing pastimes are aware that 'we are what we play'. Self-image and self-worth are bolstered by little victories. Helping customers achieve little victories in the world of the mundane is what the Delight Factor is all about.

Sports

As we shall see in Chapter 6, customer roles can be categorised as:

- Passive receptor.
- Inter-active spectator.
- Solo participant.
- Team participant.

Sport provides countless opportunities to play all of these roles. Across the world there is a move away from the spectator to the participant role. This is due, in part, to the influence of television which creates not only an awareness of an ever-increasing range of sports, but also enables the passive receptor to practice with top professionals in the privacy of the home. Sports programmes on television and training videos on specific sporting skills have transformed this hedonistic industry.

The main contribution which providers of sporting events, equipment and stadia can teach those seeking to evoke the Delight Factor are:

- People enjoy a sense of occasion. Whether at Royal Ascot, the soccer cup final, the Open Golf Championship, or the tennis tournament at Wimbledon, what delights is not only the specific sporting activity, but the ancillary pleasures of dressing up, rubbing shoulders with the champions, and indulging in luxury food and drink.

- People enjoy reassurance and recognition. No matter how experienced a player may be, a word of encouragement when things are going well, and of reassurance that 'everyone has off days' are powerful tools for enhancing performance and giving delight. When it comes to recognition, the winner's ribbon can give as much delight as a cash prize. Those in mundane industries can under-estimate the potency of symbols of recognition, whether in terms of membership of a 'club' for regular customers, or a congratulations card at the appropriate time.

- People enjoy fair play. We all have an innate sense of fairness which comes into play when we experience or witness a lack of fair play. Witnessing the joy of others can stimulate joy in ourselves. Equally, when we witness unfairness in respect of others we share it, thus blocking the release of the Delight Factor, even if we have been well treated.

Sports can bring out the best and the worst in people. There are therefore a number of negative lessons which those in other industries can seek to avoid:

- Association with undesirable customers can repel desired customers. This has been the misfortune of soccer in England and of other sports, such as greyhound racing and boxing.

- Bad behaviour overshadows good behaviour. Whether as a spectator or participant, tolerance of bad behaviour by a sports provider is perceived as a barrier to enjoyment, keeping delight at bay, despite evidence of good behaviour.

- Personality influences perceptions of performance. Although a player may be highly proficient in a game, his or her personality may stifle the Delight Factor. This phenomenon can be seen at work in other spheres. The lesson for those engaged in mundane activities is to use their behaviour to counteract the chore element experienced by customers.

Tourism

This has been the fastest growing hedonistic industry since the 1960s. Despite occasional hiccups due to wars and terrorist activities, it will continue to grow at an increasing rate into the third millennium.

Tourism is the voluntary change of location to enhance the pleasure of the traveller. Tourists experience various types of delight:

- The *delight of the new*. This comes from experiencing places, people, customs, food and drink for the first time.
- The *delight of the imagined*. This comes from experience matching or surpassing what the individual imagined it could be.
- The *delight of the familiar*. This occurs when places are revisited and continue to delight.
- The *delight of the rediscovered*. This stems from revisiting a place with someone who is visiting it for the first time and seeing it through fresh eyes.
- The *delight of the unknown*. This is not simply experiencing the new, it is embarking on an experience which one does not know the outcome.
- The *delight of the unexpected*. This occurs when reality contradicts negative preconceptions of the 'I'm sure I won't like this' type.

These six types of delight can be transferred with benefit from the hedonistic to the mundane. There are, however, certain negative characteristics of the tourist industry which others should avoid like the plague:

- False expectations.
- Cultural confusion.
- Kitsch experiences.

People embark on vacation as a means of life enhancement; they are on a flight from the mundane. As with any type of life enhancement, the tourist is predisposed to high expectations of delight. When these expectations are not fulfiled, the tourist can suffer from a greater degree of disappointment than would be the case with unfulfilled expectations of the mundane. For this reason the providers of tourism need to influence a level of expectations which is sufficiently high to attract customers, but is also deliverable. The road to bankruptcy in tourism is paved with selling false expectations.

Cultural confusion arises when tourist centres strive to satisfy the need for the new with the familiar. Fish and chip shops in Spain, *bier kellers* in Morocco, and Scottish restaurants in Zimbabwe are examples of incongruity which confuse rather than delight the customer. There is benefit to be obtained from projecting a sense of consistency in the experiences offered to customers. Striving to be all things to all people will inhibit the impact of the Delight Factor.

Kitsch is generally used to describe tawdry and cheap goods which exploit a lack of aesthetic appreciation on the part of the customer. 'Souvenirs' from holiday resorts and tourist centres often come within the category of kitsch. Experiences can also be kitsch in their nature. Pseudo-national evenings, folk dancers in night clubs, or experiencing what it feels like to be a 'native' are all examples of tawdry events which can result in disenchantment and the fleeing of delight.

Conclusion

The delight-makers are blenders of fact and fantasy, the ancient and the avant garde, the physical and psychological. Their *raison d'etre* is to amuse and astonish, to bring joy and pleasure in a context of commerce and business. Most pleasure in life is derived from the metaphysical, from giving and receiving pleasure spontaneously rather than as the outcome of a business plan. Nevertheless, when it comes to customer care the context is commercial, the environment is competitive, and the reward is profit.

Each of the major hedonistic industries provides signposts on the diverse routes to evoking delight and persuading people to pay for the experience. The basic process is:

- Arouse interest.
- Engage attention.
- Evoke absorption.
- Transform the experience.
- Transcend the expected.

The challenge for those in the more mundane industries is to adopt and adapt the process in ways which will enable their customers to enjoy the hedonistic experiences which hitherto have been the prerogative of the delight-makers. It is to this challenge that we now turn.

Chapter 6

Managing the Hedonistic Experience

Introduction

When it comes to hedonistic experiences, the customer needs to make some contribution to their success. At the very least, heart and mind must be receptive to the experience. Even the proverbial 'couch potato' has to keep awake if he or she expects to be entertained by television. The golfer has to acquire the skills of selecting and handling appropriate clubs if the game is to be enjoyed to the full. The opera lover familiar with the subtler nuances of the musical score is likely to be more delighted (or disgusted) by the performance of the orchestra and singers than the individual who believes he or she has 'no ear for music'.

To manage hedonistic experiences successfully it is necessary to be aware, not only of the roles which a customer can play, but also of the importance of frequency, duration and location in shaping the Delight Factor.

Customer Roles

There are a number of roles in which the customer contributes to a hedonistic encounter, that point of delivery where pleasure provider and customer interact. These roles, as we have seen, are:

- Passive receptor.
- Inter-active spectator.

- Solo participant.
- Team participant.

The role of passive receptor makes few demands on the customer. Watching a soap opera or a run-of-the-mill film requires little more than the suspension of belief and the ability to keep awake. Passive viewing, reading or listening may result in delight, but the experience is very one-sided; the provider putting in all the effort while the customer simply sits back and takes what is coming. It is difficult to gauge the reactions of the passive receptor since the hedonistic experience often takes place in isolation from the provider, and some time after the instrument of pleasure has been created. Films are seen long after they were made in a studio; books may have been written centuries before they were read.

There are three main measures of success in pleasing the passive receptor: the quantitative one of profit, and qualitative ones of recommendation from either the customers' 'pathfinder' – a critic – or, preferably, word-of-mouth from those who have enjoyed the experience and want others to share it. The passive receptor therefore may make a marketing contribution, but will stand aside from the process which is intended to provide delight.

This is not the case with the interactive spectator. The difference between a cinema audience and a theatre audience is that the latter can convey their delight to the performers and thus influence the performance. Similarly, football fans can make or mar a sporting event by the way in which they interact with the players. Viewing a game on television may be more comfortable, but it prevents interaction, placing the viewer in the role of passive receptor no matter how much noise he or she makes. Sight-seeing on holiday, and guided tours of museums, are pleasure-giving activities which are enriched if there are opportunities to interact with a guide.

The interactive role makes some demands on customers. This may be as simple as knowing not to clap until the end of a symphony, or as intricate as learning all aspects of the game of cricket or sumo wrestling in order to show appreciation at the proper time. Advances in telecommunications provide increasing opportunities to move from passive receptor to interactive spectator. Phone-in television and radio programmes, computer games, and *karaoke* (which means 'empty orchestra') videos which respond to personal attempts to emulate famous singers in the privacy of one's home are all examples of electronic interaction.

Interaction is dependent on the customer responding to the process of pleasure-giving; participation as a 'player' makes the customer the process. Many sports and pastimes completely involve the customer as either a solo or team player. Dancing, playing a musical instrument, keeping fit, and painting are all pleasurable experiences which the customer begins, sustains and ends. In this sense the customer is self-serving, but to optimise the pleasure it is usually necessary to go through a learning phase. The hedonistic provider in self-service experiences usually performs three roles:

- Initiating the customer into how to benefit most from the experience.
- Providing the appropriate equipment and accommodation required.
- Clearing away the aftermath of the experience.

A gourmet meal requires a knowledge of how best to please the eye, nose and palate by combinations of food and wine. In this regard, the restaurateur may need to initiate the customer into the merits of various menus. Once ordered, the food and wine must be properly prepared and served in the appropriate dishes and glasses and the correct cutlery must be to hand, as must the right atmosphere for maximum enjoyment of the meal. Between courses and after the meal the aftermath must be cleared in a manner which does not disturb the customers.

At each phase, initiation, provisioning and clearing, there will be opportunities to strengthen or dilute the Delight Factor. The initial phase in any hedonistic experience needs careful handling; assumptions of the customer's knowledge, desires and expectations must be tested sensitively. Provision of the tangible and intangible elements necessary to give pleasure calls for sound planning, ingenuity and specialist skills. Clearing the aftermath may well call for a high tolerance for dealing with the detritus of the human condition when at play.

Regardless of whether the role is receptor, spectator or participator, there are two ways in which customers may react to any hedonistic experience – as advocate or detractor. Unlike mundane services, when customers may react to an experience in a neutral fashion, or show indifference as long as nothing goes wrong, when it comes to the hedonistic, customers experience either pleasure or displeasure. A dry cleaners may be described by a customer as being 'all right'; but to describe a film, play, or sporting event in the same terms is to condemn it. Customers who consistently have a satisfactory hedonistic experience become advocates, while those who do not enjoy the experience become detractors. When it comes to assessing pleasure there are no neutrals; 'damning with faint praise' can be as damaging as loud criticism.

Frequency of the Hedonistic Experience

Jaded palates, wearied bodies, and numbed senses are just some of the effects of over-indulgence in life's pleasures. The economic law of diminishing returns has its psychic equivalent in the law of diminishing delight. When pleasures become commonplace they join the mundane; enjoyment becomes boredom, delight dilutes to pretence. Just as keeping up appearances can lead to economic bankruptcy, so too can pretended pleasure lead to psychological decay.

In day-to-day living, diversions tend to occur more frequently than delight enhancers. We look forward to reading our daily paper, seeing our weekly sporting event, visiting the theatre once a quarter, or preparing for our annual vacation. Other occasions for rejoicing can be less frequent – a golden wedding, a centenary celebration, or entering a new millennium. The less frequent, the higher expectations will be. Companies providing a Delight Factor, therefore, have to master 'expectations creep' by controlling the rate at which customers' expectations progress.

We can see 'expectations creep' at work in film series where increasingly sophisticated special effects are used to attract return visits by those who have seen earlier films in the series. Restaurants manage 'expectations creep' by changing their menus or providing small surprises such as a free aperitif. The key factor in 'expectations creep' is pacing; surprises must be brought into the hedonistic experience at a rate which is comfortable to the customer. Too many surprises cause confusion, too few result in boredom, and either way the Delight Factor is damaged.

Another danger associated with the timing of pleasurable events is hedonistic overload, or in simpler terms, 'too much of a good thing'. As children we are eager to take a trip on the roller coaster immediately after indulging in the delights of hamburgers and milkshakes. When we grow older we may think we are wiser, but hospitals are full of sufferers from hedonistic overload. It might be claimed that adults are responsible for the consequences of their pleasures, but increasingly, the law suggests otherwise. Barmen are sued by drunks in the United States; companies are being held responsible for contributing to hedonistic overload. While this has to be taken into account by providers, there is another aspect of overloading which is in danger of snuffing out the Delight Factor. This is the provision of hedonistic packages put together using different types of pleasure experiences.

A typical example is to fly from London to Egypt by Concorde, visit the Pyramids, see an open air production of Aida, go shopping in the souk, attend a gourmet dinner of Arabian delicacies and be back in London within the space of three days. Even the most robust participant is unlikely to sustain a sense of delight throughout such a trip. Hedonistic packages are here to stay, but they have to be designed so that the pacing and congruency of the pleasurable experiences result in the emotions and senses being enjoyably stimulated rather than uncomfortably sated.

Duration of the Hedonistic Experience

Delight is determined by the nature, frequency and duration of the hedonistic experience. Unless these three are in harmony the Delight Factor will not come into operation. Pleasure ended prematurely withers into anti-climax; extended too long it degenerates into pain.

Diversions tend to have a shorter life-span than 'Life Enhancers'. A comedy sketch can be enjoyed in seconds, a game of golf cannot be played in less time than it takes to cover nine or eighteen holes. Half an hour may suffice to view a television programme, but it is unlikely to be sufficient time to view the treasures of a national art gallery.

The duration of a hedonistic experience by a customer is determined by one or more of the following:

- Physical endurance.
- Emotional strength.
- Convention.
- Tradition.
- Natural phenomena.
- Cost.
- Medium.
- Repeatability.

There are physical limits to how long one can play a game, watch a film, or listen to music without the body succumbing to fatigue. When the hedonistic experience is associated with risk, such as hang-gliding or water-skiing, the nature of the risk can impose limits on how long an individual should be exposed to it.

The dancing marathons of the 1930s epitomised in the film *They Shoot Horses Don't They?* provide a graphic example of a pleasure-giving pursuit – ballroom dancing – becoming a source of agony and despair when it is too extended.

Emotional turmoil can arise when the hedonistic experience calls forth conflicting emotions. Whether on the screen, stage or printed page, there is a finite number of emotions which we can cope with at any one time. Experiences which evoke joy and sadness together with feelings of uplift and foreboding can lead to mental disorders and reduce our capacity to enjoy life. Those whose aim is to divert or enhance need to be wary of being drawn into the dark swamps of exploitation.

Convention – unwritten rules – can dictate the duration of hedonistic events. Cocktail parties (for some people a source of pleasure) should last about two hours to be considered a success. A half-hour play is unlikely to qualify as an enjoyable evening out, though it could be perceived as a pleasurable event on television. Too rigid an adherence to convention can dilute the hedonistic experience; equally, to ignore it can lead to unfulfilled expectations.

Tradition is a twin of convention. Some traditions have a wider sphere of influence than others when it comes to pleasurable events. Christmas is expected to be celebrated over a period of days rather than hours. The Wimbledon tennis tournament lasts two weeks, and a wedding breakfast takes hours rather than minutes. As with convention, a break with tradition can either strengthen or dilute the Delight Factor. Change should be seen as a calculated risk.

Natural phenomena determine the length of such hedonistic pursuits as skiing, mountaineering and, on a more mundane level, barbecues and picnics. The Delight Factor arising from an open air concert can be washed away by a sudden shower.

Just as cost is a limiting factor in most aspects of life, so with hedonistic companies. Their aim is to make a profit, therefore the duration of an event will be determined by the revenue expected from the customers *vis a vis* the costs of staging such an event. Equally, the price paid by the customer will create expectations of the duration should this not be stated at the outset. Visits to a theme park or zoo are expected to last the best part of a day, whereas a visit to the theatre which lasts more than three hours is a rare occurrence.

The medium involved in providing the hedonistic experience influences its duration. The time spent reading a novel is set by the reader, and video recording machines make it possible to employ self-pacing in viewing a recorded programme. The time span of a theatrical event can not be self-paced, nor can the period of spectator sports. Self-pacing gives added value to a hedonistic experience. For this reason providers have to be fully aware of the limitations and advantages of various media.

Repeatability is important in determining the duration of any hedonistic experience. The easier it is to repeat the experience, the shorter its duration can be. Customers will spend less time on a visit to a local museum than they will to one which is in a place they are unlikely to re-visit. The 'Ultimate Event' concerts of Frank Sinatra, Liza Minelli and Sammy Davis, Jr. in the late 1980s were sell-outs, not simply because of the quality of the performance, but because of the likelihood that they would not be repeated. The 'once in a lifetime' label can literally add a sense of uniqueness, but it is also likely to raise expectations which, if not fulfiled or surpassed, will lead to bitter disappointment with no opportunity for the provider to recover the situation.

Location of the Hedonistic Experience

Location is a key factor in shaping a hedonistic experience. For any hedonistic company, consideration has to be given to a range of options such as:

- Customer's home.
- Customer's choice.

- Fixed location.
- Mobile.
- Single location.
- Multiple location.
- Exotic location.

Of all the commercial hedonistic experiences in the home, watching television is the most common. As mentioned in Chapter 2, a survey conducted by *Radio Times* in 1991 revealed insights into viewing habits in Britain. Few people view television without engaging in some other activity, ranging from eating to making love. Forty-five per cent of those surveyed claimed that they read while viewing. Reading, like listening to the radio or recordings, can be enjoyed in any location of a person's choosing.

Other pleasurable experiences are confined to fixed locations. There is only one place where you can enjoy the thrill of the Eiffel Tower; the same holds good for all other tourist sites. To enjoy opera live, the customer has to visit an Opera House; athletics take place in fixed locations, as do other sporting events. Sources of pleasure such as painting and sculpture can be moved from one location to another without damaging the hedonistic experience of the spectator. Holiday resorts are fixed in single locations, though Disney World shows that theme parks can be replicated. There is only one Paris Ritz, but there are thousands of McDonalds.

Location in itself is often part of the Delight Factor – the view from a hotel room can be more important than the decor or the food. Ease of access to other desired locations plays an important role in influencing customers' perceptions of a hotel, restaurant or shopping mall.

Perhaps the most significant trend in location is the increasing penchant for the exotic or bizarre. The performing of Hamlet in Elsinore Castle, floating hotels, and restaurants at the top of towers have all been with us for some time. More recently, as mentioned in Chapter 5, museums, zoos, and battleships have made their facilities available for hire by those wanting to celebrate in unusual locations. From oceans to the stratosphere, new locations are being explored by those who want to provide something new for the pleasure seekers.

No matter how exotic or mundane may be the location there is one common thread: the Delight Factor must be managed, but in a different way from traditional management.

The Battlefields of Customer Care

It is fashionable to describe continuous improvement in service quality as a never-ending journey. While there is truth in that analogy, it can result in demotivation if staff envisage an endless road before them. The spurt on the initial miles, stimulated by some quality improvement programme, slows down as momentum is lost to other priorities. Eventually the once interesting walk gives way to a trudge of apathy, often resulting in a complete halt as enthusiasm wanes and roads to other goals cause diversions.

A more accurate metaphor is that of a battlefield. Service quality which results in customer satisfaction is the outcome of inspired leadership, clearly defined strategy, innovative tactics, careful training and deployment of human resources, up-to-date equipment, and unfailing support for those in the firing line.

Using the metaphor of battlefields draws out the point that to ensure customer satisfaction it is necessary to fight on several fronts simultaneously. There will be reverses, and some initiatives will be thwarted; certain people will fight more effectively than others. Above all, victory can not be taken for granted – one must be ever on one's guard to espy lurking threats and emerging opportunities. To hold the field of battle it is necessary to win over and retain the commitment of management, the enthusiasm of all employees, and the allegiance of customers.

Winning Commitment

Before considering a strategy for optimising customer satisfaction, certain pre-conditions must exist among the managers who will be leading their troops into battle:

- Determination to establish and sustain a service quality supremacy in each selected battlefield.
- Acceptance of the inter-dependency of strategy, cultural systems and behaviour in the fight to capture the hearts and minds of employees, customers and other stakeholders.
- Awareness of the need to pursue continuous attitude/behaviour training which will keep morale high even in the toughest battle.

Unless managers are determined that the prime criterion for measuring their performance is the level of customer satisfaction, they will be unable to display the inspired leadership essential for winning battles. Such determination does not come easily. Initially, there will be difficulties in perceiving a motivational shift from 'satisfying the boss' to 'satisfying the customer'. It will take some time to convince more junior staff (and even some managers) that the best route to satisfying the boss is to satisfy the customer.

Achieving high levels of customer satisfaction calls for a blending of new and traditional competences for both managers and staff.

Managers need to be proficient in four fairly new areas of competence:

- *Empowerment* – the ability to enable individuals to acquire the competence and confidence to use their initiative within a prescribed area.
- *Evangelising* – the ability to communicate a message in a way which motivates listeners and gains their commitment to the speaker's values and beliefs.

- *Opportunity Mapping* – the ability to identify opportunities to delight and take swift action to seize them, thus gaining competitive advantage.
- *Trend Scanning* – the ability to monitor developments relevant to an industry, identifying those which will require changes of some kind and planning accordingly.

These competences carry in their wake implications for management style and practices. Table 6.1 specifies these implications.

Staff at all levels require in addition to proficiency in the job at hand, four new clusters of competence if the company is to win the battle for leadership in customer care:

- *Needs Anticipation* – the ability to foresee and take action to meet both physical and psychic needs of customers. This links with the capabilities of managers in the areas of empowerment, trend scanning and opportunity mapping.

- *Expectations Gate-keeping* – the ability to stimulate and control expectations by influencing the expectation threshold of customers at critical stages in the customer-provider relationship. This links with the capability of managers to evangelise in a manner which enthuses, but does not engender false hopes.

- *Perception Shaping* – the ability to influence the way in which the customer sees a situation and acts accordingly. This links with the proficiency of managers in opportunity mapping and evangelising.

- *Time Shaping* – the ability to help customers shape their time the way they want it. This skill was described in Chapter 2. It is very much a function of empowerment.

These competences and their use in managing the Delight Factor are summarised in Table 6.2.

TABLE 6.1
COMPETENCES FOR MANAGING DELIGHT

Competence	Implications for Management Style and Practices
Empowerment – the ability to enable individuals to acquire the competence to use their initiative within a prescribed area.	– Encourage openness and trust in relationships. – Be seen as a source of support and guidance. – Empower to empower. – Be psychologically prepared for things going wrong. – Regularly review and, if possible, increase the scope of empowerment.
Evangelising – the ability to communicate a message in a manner which motivates the listeners and gains their commitment to the speaker's values and beliefs.	– Keep the customer care message fresh. – Regularly reassure staff that the concepts of service and care are noble callings. – Use as many media as possible to spread the gospel. – Be seen to practice what you preach. – Build up a cadre of disciples across the organisation.

(/cont'd....)

TABLE 6.1
COMPETENCES FOR MANAGING DELIGHT

Competence	Implications for Management Style and Practices
Opportunity Mapping – the ability to identify opportunities and take swift action to seize them, so gaining competitive advantage.	– Be aware of the boundaries with which the company interacts. – Adopt variable time horizons for planning. – Provide alternative paths for reaching desired goals. – Prepare path finding expeditions before committing significant resources. – Keep map regularly up-dated.
Trend Scanning – the ability to monitor developments relevant to an industry, identifying those which will require changes of some kind and planning accordingly.	– Keep informed through market research and media analysis. – Be sensitive to weak signals which could increase in strength. – Keep abreast of competitors' activity. – Be sufficiently flexible in planning processes to enable swift adaptation to change. – Be clear on whether the strategic preference is to be 'first there' or 'me too'.

TABLE 6.2
COMPETENCES TO DELIGHT

Competence	Delight Factor Opportunities
Needs Anticipation – the ability to foresee and take action to meet the emerging needs of customers.	– Physical needs: *Product/Service availability* *Product/Service reliability* *Product/Service durability* *Product/Service flexibility.* – Psychological needs: *Reassurance* *Enhanced self-esteem* *Desired level of social contact* *Congruency of values* *Achievement* *Trust* *Understanding* *Recognition.* – Spiritual needs: *Environmental awareness* *Community awareness* *Waste avoidance* *Helping the disadvantaged.*

(cont'd....)

TABLE 6.2
COMPETENCES TO DELIGHT

Competence	Delight Factor Opportunities
Expectations Gate-keeping – the ability to stimulate and control expectations by influencing the expectations threshold of customers at critical states in the customer-provider relationship.	– Inspire customer by appearance and approach. – Adjust level of expectations threshold by keeping customer up-dated on progress. – Exceed expectations in some way, no matter how small. – Help customer redirect expectations if unmovable barriers exist. – Continuously seek out expectations of customers and adjust to changes. – Use existing customers to influence expectations of new customers. – Check that customers' expectations have been met or exceeded.

Perception Shaping – the ability to influence the way in which the customer sees a situation and acts accordingly.	– Sharpen perception by clear communication of relevant situational factors.
	– Broaden perception by providing options.
	– Be aware of effects of stereotyping and take action to overcome it.
	– Distinguish between situations which are:
	   Life changing
	   Life enhancing
	   Life maintaining
	– Always remember that perception is reality.

(cont'd...)

TABLE 6.2
COMPETENCES TO DELIGHT

Competence	Delight Factor Opportunities
Time-shaping – the ability to help customers shape their time the way they want it.	– Use a range of time-shapers rather than relying on speed alone. – Identify the psychic time zone within which customer is operating. – Identify likely positive and negative time states influencing customer. Take action to reinforce the positive and eliminate the negative. – Forewarn customer of changes in time-scales, deadlines, etc. – Assist customer to be "time conscious" and cooperate in reaping the benefits of Time-shaping.

Windows of Opportunity for Delight

In every industry there are a number of windows of opportunity which enable the flame of delight to shine through. The essence of managing the Delight Factor is to make the fullest use of each window, such as:

- Product range.
- Cleanliness.
- Convenience.
- Service.
- Flexibility.
- Comfort.
- Ambience.

Table 6.3 gives examples of windows of opportunity for such industries as:

- Airlines.
- Banks.
- Cinemas.
- Department stores.
- Supermarkets.
- Hotels.
- Restaurants.

These examples are intended to stimulate thinking about the windows which exist in many industries, but may have been bricked up by lack of thought or managerial incompetence. Before the Delight Factor can be managed, these blockages must be removed.

TABLE 6.3
WINDOWS OF OPPORTUNITY FOR DELIGHT

Industry	Windows	Opportunity for Delight
Airlines	Safety	– Providing reassurance without heightening anxiety. – Making safety drills interesting.
	Convenience	– Scheduling that reduces door-to-door journey times. – Ease of check-in. – Efficiency of baggage handling.
	Service	– Personalising customer care. – Sensitive handling of special cases.
	Value	– Providing discounts for related services. – Attaching minimal conditions to use of ticket.
	Flexibility	– Helpful response to customer's change of plans. – Willingness to adapt to changed circumstances.
Banks	Security	– Discreet use of safety devices on premises. – Reassurance on safety of financial procedures and deposits.
	Service	– Ready response to special needs. – Customer-friendly systems and staff.
	Convenience	– Ease of access to premises and direct/indirect contact with the appropriate official. – Contact hours.

(cont'd....)

TABLE 6.3
WINDOWS OF OPPORTUNITY FOR DELIGHT

Industry	Windows	Opportunity for Delight
Banks	Value	– Competitiveness of rates of interest and charges. – Extent of psychic added-value.
	Product range	– Innovative bundling of products. – Distinctive product features.
Cinema	Entertainment	– Impact of film on customer. – Enjoyment of support features, e.g. trailers.
	Comfort	– Design and layout of seating. – Quality of sound and light.
	Security	– Discreet monitoring of audience and quick action to deal with unruly customers.
	Convenience	– Location. – Ease of parking.
	Value	– Innovative pricing. – Cost of food/drink purchased on the premises.
Department Store	Ambience	– Welcoming atmosphere. – Attractive layout.
	Product Range	– Variety of products. – Availability of unusual products.

(cont'd....)

TABLE 6.3
WINDOWS OF OPPORTUNITY FOR DELIGHT

Industry	Windows	Opportunity for Delight
Department Store	Service	– Friendly efficiency. – Product and layout knowledge of staff.
	Value	– Prices appropriate to customer's perception of type of store. – Significant psychic added-value associated with high priced products.
	Convenience	– Ability for customer to meet wide range of needs in same location. – Ease of payment and of transport of goods.
Super-markets	Product range	– Variety of products and brands. – Availability of unusual products.
	Cleanliness	– Visible signs of attention to all aspects of hygiene. – Freshness of decoration and equipment.
	Convenience	– Ease of access and layout. – Ease of check-out and loading/unloading.
	Value	– Competitive bundling of products. – Special promotions and discounts.
	Service	– Spontaneity of help. – Product and layout knowledge of staff.
	Facilities	– Specialist assistance for children, the very old and others with special needs.

(cont'd....)

TABLE 6.3
WINDOWS OF OPPORTUNITY FOR DELIGHT

Industry	Windows	Opportunity for Delight
Hotels	Cleanliness	– Visible signs of hygiene awareness. – Freshness of decoration and furnishings.
	Comfort	– Ambience conducive to relaxation. – Furniture and fittings designed for comfort and convenience of customer.
	Service	– Discreet attentiveness. – Personalisation at a level desired by the customer.
	Value	– No hidden extras. – Special rates for special needs.
	Facilities	– Range of recreational and business facilities readily available. – Specialist staff can cope with special requests.
Restaurants	Ambience	– Surroundings appropriate to type of meals provided. – Welcoming atmosphere at all times.
	Food	– Quality and quantity appropriate to customer's needs. – Novelty in nature, preparation and presentation at a level with which the customer is comfortable.
	Service	– Discreet attentiveness. – Pace appropriate to customer's needs.

(cont'd...)

TABLE 6.3
WINDOWS OF OPPORTUNITY FOR DELIGHT

Industry	Windows	Opportunity for Delight
Restaurants	Value	– No hidden extras. – Options sufficient to permit significant variation in prices.
	Convenience	– Meals available at times customers want them. – Location adds value.
	Facilities	– All parts are manifestly clean. – Privacy is protected through layout and discreet use of background music.

How Delight is Blocked

Most barriers to using the Delight Factor can be classified into mistaken beliefs, negative feelings and organisational constraints. Those engaged directly in the provision of customer care need help in overcoming these barriers which limit entry into the realm of delight.

Mistaken beliefs affecting customer care fall into five categories:

1. Blame.
2. Dominance.
3. Idealisation.
4. Normality.
5. Objectivity.

In business and other walks of life, many of our mistaken beliefs arise from the tendency to want to allocate blame for a particular situation to oneself or others. Seeking a scapegoat for some failure in service is all too common. 'Don't blame me – it's the fault of ......'. Customers are not interested in where blame lies, they seek to have the situation remedied as soon as possible. This does not mean that establishing accountability for problems is not important. However, from the standpoint of the customer, allocation of blame should be the last step in resolving a problem, not the first.

Care has to be taken to avoid the trap of too ready an acceptance of blame (some people use this as a device to escape from finding a solution).

A spontaneous acceptance of corporate accountability (within legally approved limits) is a positive response which will help restore customer satisfaction in most situations. Acceptance of accountability needs to replace allocation of blame as a way of dealing with problems of customer care.

Dominance – the belief that might is right – has long held sway in business. It needs its twin, subservient behaviour, to survive. Beliefs associated with dominance play a large role in shaping attitudes on sexual, racial and class matters; they lie at the base of one of the major barriers to using the Delight Factor – the perception that 'service' is a synonym for 'servile'. Companies need to help their employees understand the debilitating effect which the perpetuation of the dominance-subservience axis can have in providing a service that delights. Because this acceptance of dominance has underpinned many traditional management practices, its elimination has to be carefully planned. The boosting of self-esteem and the cultivation of caring skills will be key components in the disappearance of dominance.

Idealisation is rigid adherence to values and beliefs, many of which are outmoded. It is a more difficult animal to destroy as it can appear to be a positive force, bestowing wisdom and helpfulness to a greater extent than is justified. It can be the begetter of unswerving loyalty in the face of defeat. Idealisation can stifle innovation, openness and empowerment, thus cutting off three of the essential energy sources of the Delight Factor. Idealisation needs to be replaced by constructive realism in the belief system of service companies. By this means, broad focused and sharp visioned binoculars will replace rose tinted spectacles.

Normality is the begetter of the belief that something that is widespread or generally accepted must be right. Its existence inhibits creativity and can help perpetuate unethical behaviour – 'everyone does it, why should we be different'. The Delight Factor has difficulty in surviving in an organisation which has adopted normality as part of its belief system. By its very nature, the use of the Delight Factor calls for experimenting and path-finding; normality needs to be recognised for what it is – the underpinning of the *status quo*. This belief needs to be replaced by a pioneering spirit which will foster the Delight Factor.

Objectivity is the mistaken belief that one can reach decisions on the basis of value-free facts, totally ignoring personal feelings and beliefs. History and personal experience show that such a state of affairs is impossible. In customer care situations emotional factors influence actions and reactions of both service provider and the customer. Recognising this, and equipping staff with the skills necessary to deal with it, lies at the heart of training in managing the Delight Factor.

Conclusion

Managing the Delight Factor is no easy option, but successfully doing so can bring rich rewards, both financially and psychologically.

The role of the customer is vital to the outcome, as is the management of the frequency, duration and location of the desired hedonistic experience. New and revised concepts and competences of managing service encounters have to be acquired at all levels in a company. Blockages stemming from outmoded practices and faulty thinking have to be overcome.

This need not present a major problem, often all it needs is a nudge as we shall see in the next chapter.

Chapter 7

Nudging into Delight

Introduction

Winning the jack-pot on a fruit machine sometimes requires only a nudge; so it is with giving the customer a delightful experience rather than merely a satisfactory one. Unlike the fruit machine, winning the customer over is not a matter of chance; it is the creation of circumstances which will render the customer willing to be nudged psychologically rather than physically.

The existence of delight, no matter how fleeting, depends on a fusion of internal joy and benign conditions. It is the skillful use of these conditions with which we are concerned in this chapter. We will consider around sixty 'nudges' which can be brought into play to win over customers. They are described in broad terms followed by specific examples of how they can be used best in a variety of situations.

From Accessibility to Assurance

For ease of illustration we will deal with the 'nudges' in alphabetical order; another reason for this treatment is that their relative importance varies from one industry to another.

Accessibility. Finding the right person in the right place at the right time is almost certain to be a source of delight. This is particularly so in the 'help me' industries, such as banking and medical services where customers may need assistance in dealing with a problem quickly. Partly through a lack of empowerment, and partly due to status consciousness, many customers perceive 'the right person' as being the most senior person in the company.

There is a need to wean customers from this perception by creating a culture of confidence, making every employee feel that he/she is 'the right person' for some part of the service and is aware of his/her counterparts, so that the customer's problem can be resolved swiftly. The fewer people a customer has to contact to satisfy a need, the more likely it is that he will be nudged into delight.

Added Value. This comes in many forms, tangible and intangible. What needs to be remembered is that added value is what the customer perceives it to be, not what the provider sees it to be. Unless the core product or service satisfies the customer, no amount of added value will nudge the customer into delight. For the added value nudge to be effective it is essential for the provider to establish what added value the customer would welcome. The concept of psychic added value is often neglected or over-shadowed by companies which confuse added value with give-aways and gimmicks. While these may have short-term novelty appeal, customers can soon be sated, resulting in the symbol of added value being counter productive, nudging the customer from satisfaction into dissatisfaction.

Advice. Customers seek three types of advice:

- Professional – guidance on matters with which they are unfamiliar and which require high levels of specialist knowledge.
- Quotidian – guidance on every day matters which the customer could deal with if he/she had the time or desire to do so.
- Confirmatory – guidance on matters which the customer has already dealt with or proposes to do so.

In all these cases customers judge the advice against three criteria:

- Quality – did it result in the desired outcomes?

- Manner – was it conveyed in a caring way?
- Cost – were the resulting monetary and psychic costs of receiving and acting on the advice acceptable?

Without a positive answer to all three it will not be possible to nudge the customer into delight.

Ambience. This encompasses a variety of both tangible and intangible features. While the former are self-evident in terms of premises and furnishings, they alone are unlikely to provide the nudge into delight. This requires a climate of care, affecting both the senses and the emotions. A simple five senses test can be applied to assessing the appropriateness of ambience:

- Sight – are staff appearance, and layout, decoration and the furnishing of the premises appealing to the eye?
- Sound – is the volume of background music, announcements and other sounds at levels appropriate to the mood and ages of the customers?
- Touch – are surfaces clean and the furniture comfortable; is the air conditioning or heating set at appropriate levels?
- Smell – does the air smell fresh; is there an absence of obnoxious odours?
- Taste – are all consumables attractive to the palate?

  The importance of the senses in relation to the Delight Factor is considered more fully in Chapter 8. The important point in terms of ambience is that its effects on the senses can make or destroy the creation of a 'mood' which is conducive to delight.

Anniversaries. By evoking pleasant memories of past events, these can reinforce current good experiences being enjoyed by customers, and thereby nudge them into delight. In using anniversaries as a nudge, the service provider should focus on events associated with the customer-provider relationship rather than birthdays, wedding anniversaries or other personal mile-stones. Any attempt by a company to join in celebrating such personal events may be perceived by a customer as an intrusion, resulting in a worsening of the customer-provider relationship. The more personalised the commemoration and the more it accords with the customer's values, the more effective the nudge into delight.

Appearance. This has a close connection with ambience, but with a primary focus on the image which the customer receives of the dress, personal presentation and disposition of the service provider. Customers seek a standard of appearance which meets the following criteria:

- Appropriate to the task being performed.
- Does not intimidate nor embarrass the customer.
- Clean and in good order.
- Distinguishable in emergencies.

Customers do not expect dentists to wear pin-striped suits when operating on their teeth; equally they would not expect a bank manager to be wearing a surgical suit. Service providers who are 'dressed for the job' are more likely to nudge their customers into delight than would be the case if their appearance caused confusion in the mind of the customer. Equally, where dress is chosen to create a sense of apprehension, such as the black leather coats favoured by the Gestapo, there will be little prospect of the customer feeling delight.

When it comes to personal appearance, cleanliness is next to delightfulness – enough said? Perhaps not, because of the reluctance to raise concerns about inadequate personal hygiene when it comes to colleagues. We live in an age when there is an abundance of advice and products to obviate all causes of poor personal hygiene. It is therefore essential that all involved in dealing with other people are made aware of the hygiene standards expected of them. If this cannot be achieved through sensitive handling, the issue needs to be confronted.

Uniforms, or corporate dress, are now commonplace. They can be extremely important in cases of emergency when customers can readily identify those best qualified to deal with the situation. By reinforcing role recognition uniforms can make crowd control easier. On the other hand, uniforms can have an alienating effect on customers, making it more difficult to nudge them into delight if the uniform is intimidating, as in the case of security staff who may be the first person customers meet.

Assurance. The ability to put at rest the fears and concerns of customers is one of the most effective nudges. It calls for the establishment of a rapport between provider and customer and the development of mutual trust. It is obvious that the concerns of the customer can not be set to rest if they are not known to the provider. Therefore, the more open the relationship is, the greater the chances of delight will be. Openness depends upon the ability to bring into play such factors as competence, credibility, and confidentiality. These and others are dealt with in the next section.

From Behaviour to Cycles of Service

In this chapter I am attempting to highlight a range of options for nudging customers from feeling satisfied to feeling delighted. Some of the items covered are broad-based, while others are sharply focused; each can be brought together with others to create a winning combination.

Behaviour. Because it is so all-embracing we may fail to recognise that behaviour can be planned, selected and directed to achieve precise objectives. Behaviour is everything we say and everything we do. We can choose our behaviour just as we can choose our clothes; as with clothes, our behaviour should be appropriate to the occasion. When it comes to delighting the customer, the behaviour of the service provider needs to:

- Put the customer at ease.
- Convey genuine care for the customer's needs.

- Help the customer to meet his/her needs in a manner which will result in delight.

A warm smile, a gentle touch and reassuring words are all behavioural nudges. In seeking to use them effectively, we should always keep in mind that too weak a nudge may be no nudge at all, and that too strong a nudge may become an unacceptable push.

Bonding. Customer retention is usually the reward of customer care. By providing an experience of delight which the customer wants to repeat, the service provider creates a bond of mutual benefit. Regular customers are already likely to be satisfied; while care needs to be taken to sustain satisfaction, the effort needed to nudge them into delight will be smaller than with new customers. The bonding process takes time and can be effected in many ways, including:

- Special discounts and other financial incentives.
- Priority in acquiring goods; making reservations.
- Provision of 'free gifts'.
- Early notification of special events.
- Access to restricted areas.

Whatever its form, bonding should enhance the self-worth of the customer, bestowing a sense of 'special treatment' which results in delight.

Care. Like behaviour this is a very broad topic which can manifest itself in many ways. In the final analysis, however, it must create in the minds of customers a sense of genuine concern for their well-being if it is to nudge them into delight. There are different categories of care:

- Personal care is that directly experienced by the customer.
- Vicarious care is that witnessed by the customer.
- Tough care is that which is in the customer's best interest, though it does not comply with his/her immediate wants.

Within each category there exist many different ways in which care can be expressed. Personal care can be expressed by 'staying with' a customer until his/her needs have been fully met. Vicarious care can be shown by the manner in which, say, an elderly patient is seen to be looked after in a nursing home. Tough care reveals itself by refusing a loan which the customer would find great difficulty in repaying. Whatever its category, care provides a major nudge into delight.

Codes. By themselves, explicit statements of actions which will guide the behaviour of service providers will not act as a nudge. However, in complying with codes (or charters or contracts) the ground is prepared for action which can tip the scales in favour of delight.

Communications. The more thoroughly we understand what the customer wants, and the more clearly that we explain how best we can help, the better the chance of nudging the customer into delight will be. There are, therefore, three skills to be mastered by the service provider:

- Listening.
- Talking.
- Writing.

In each case there are few simple guidelines which, if followed, will almost certainly delight the customer. When listening you should:

- Let customers finish speaking; do not rush them nor end their sentences.
- Encourage customers to reveal their needs, expectations and concerns by asking 'open' questions. For example, rather than ask 'Did you receive our brochure?', phrase the question, 'What did you think of our brochure?'
- Concentrate on what is being said – not on what you plan to say next.
- Take notes if necessary.

- Be sensitive to body language.
- Summarise what has been said from time-to-time to ensure that you and the customer are on the same wavelength.

When talking to the customer remember to:

- Ask question to find out needs, expectations and concerns.
- Offer a choice where possible. For example, would the customer prefer to have documents posted or come to collect them.
- Point out possible outcomes; spare the customer unpleasant surprises.
- Be accurate – don't guess. Offer to check the facts and get back to the customer.
- Use everyday language – avoid jargon.

Finally, the following tips in writing can change your letter from one that satisfies to one that delights:

- Before putting pen to paper, think carefully of what "writing tone" is best suited to both the subject matter and the customer. Wherever possible inject warmth and friendliness into your writing.
- Write short sentences and paragraphs.
- Use words the customer will understand – always try to express rather than impress.
- Remember that customers will misinterpret anything that can be misinterpreted.
- Customers will 'read between the lines', so be careful what you leave unsaid.

Competence. Customers expect high levels of competence on the part of those supplying service. There are five competences which are particularly significant in managing the Delight Factor:

- Product knowledge.
- Interpersonal skills.
- Retrieval skills.
- Option development.
- Limitation awareness.

Product knowledge encompasses a depth of knowledge about key products and services together with an awareness of the sources of expertise which can be made available to the customer. Interpersonal skills are those required to establish effective and caring relationships with customers; many of these are covered in this chapter.

The next three skills clusters are less well known, but are just as important in ensuring competent performance. Retrieval skills are necessary for coping when things go wrong. The ability to retrieve a situation can result in delight if the retrieval process runs swiftly and smoothly. Option development is the ability to provide the customer with choices. Options can cover not only the core products, but methods of payment, delivery dates and so forth. The more options available to the customer the greater will be a sense of personalised service. Limitation awareness is closely related to empowerment (see Chapter 6). Service providers need to be aware of their limitations in terms of:

- Discretion in handling special cases.
- Accountability.
- Commitment of the company.
- Retrieval.

No matter how extensively empowerment is practised there will always be some limits on individual initiative. When setting limits the aim should be to encourage staff to view the limits as providing optimum space for individual initiative, not prison walls to impede freedom of action. Service providers need such space if they are to nudge the customer into delight.

Complaints Handling. All complaints are signals of a lack of delight; all complaints offer opportunities to create delight. Complaints can arise from a variety of causes:

- Malfunction of the product/service.
- Unrealistic expectations of customers.
- Inter-personal problems between providers and customers.
- Broken promises.
- Misuse by the customer.
- Deliberate awkwardness by the customer.

No matter the cause, the handling of the complaint should follow a well tested formula:

- Be perceived as a problem-solver, not as a problem receiver. From the outset do get across to the customer your willingness to help.
- Project a sense of care. Even if it should prove not possible to resolve the problem to the complete satisfaction of the customer, it is always possible to convey a sympathetic attitude by choice of words and manner.
- Get the facts. Cut through the tangle of emotional under-growth which can often hide the reality of the problem.
- Describe the action you will take to handle the complaint, giving some indication of the likely time-span.
- Provide regular feedback on progress, particularly if the issues are complex and it will take some time to reach a conclusion.

Confidentiality. There are a number of situations where the law requires, or customers expect, their affairs to be handled in the strictest confidence. This particularly pertains to financial and medical matters; in such cases there is no scope to nudge the customer into delight – though breaches of confidence will have serious consequences.

Nudges are possible in situations where the customer seeks to spring a pleasant surprise on someone and achieves this with the co-operation of the service provider. Typical situations are delivering flowers or some other token of affection, providing the surprise birthday cake at just the right moment, or assisting in the unexpected presentation of an award. In such cases, the Delight Factor is doubly effective since its impact is shared by both donor and recipient. On the other hand, the premature revelation of an intended surprise will extinguish delight for all concerned.

Cycles of Service. When the service process runs smoothly from the time when the customer states a need to the time when the need is fully satisfied, it can nudge the customer into delight. Cycles of service may be of a very short duration, or extend over days or even weeks. The service provider can enhance the possibility of delight by adjusting the speed of the cycle to match the customer's needs:

- Eliminate any unnecessary stages in the cycle, particularly those with a high chore content.
- Complete the cycle in a seamless manner.

From Delivery to Follow-through

The ability to nudge into delight is determined as much by the manner in which service providers go about their business as by the outcome. This is highlighted in this section.

Delivery. The delivery of a service may be at one fixed location (e.g., a nursing home) or many locations (e.g., bank branches) or the home of the customer; it may be wholly automated (e.g., cash dispenser) or totally personal (e.g., hairdressing). Whatever the circumstances, it is at the point of delivery where delight is kindled or snuffed out.

Diversions. Providing customers with activities which distract them from any negative aspects of service delivery, such as queuing, can act as an effective nudge. The effectiveness of the nudge will depend on whether the customer perceives the diversion to be aimed at enhancing his/her comfort level or exploiting the situation for purely sales purposes.

If it is the latter, it can have an adverse effect on customer satisfaction. For example, the habit of cinemas holding a so-called 'intermission' prior to the feature film simply to entice customers to buy sweets and drinks does not increase the entertainment value for those film-goers whose objective is to see the film, rather than noisily consume junk food.

Empathy. This can be a major nudge if the customer perceives that the service provider is making a genuine effort to get on the same wavelength in order to help achieve the customer's goal.

Endurance. By being willing to stay with the customer despite frustration and/or difficult demands, it is possible to nudge even the most awkward customer into delight. However, endurance has to be tempered by attention to the needs of other customers who may be more reticent in articulating their demands. Nor should endurance be at the cost of suffering abuse or anti-social behaviour from the customer.

Enterprise. Delight can result from the customer perceiving initiative by the service provider which goes beyond what is expected.

Exclusiveness. Appealing to the desire for a distinctive self-identity or for enhanced status through association with an elite can be an effective nudge. Gaining membership of a much-sought-after club, wearing designer clothes, or purchasing an unique work of art can all result in a move into delight for those who gain satisfaction from that regrettable, but wide-spread trait – snobbishness.

Fairness. This is an elusive concept. Its success as a nudge depends on the creation of a win-win outcome which more than satisfies the customer.

Feedback. Keeping a customer fully informed about the progress of a transaction can be a useful nudge. Similarly, checking customer satisfaction subsequent to the delivery of goods and services is a powerful device for sparking the Delight Factor.

Flexibility. Displaying a willingness to adapt to the changing circumstances of the customer is one of the strongest nudges which the service provider can bring into play.

Follow-through. In a world where everyone delivered the action promised to the customer and ensured completion in accordance with the customer's needs and expectations, this would not be an effective nudge. Unfortunately, we do not live in such a world. Therefore, there is real competitive advantage to be gained by demonstrating effective follow-through.

From Games to Juggling

Fun and delight are close bed-fellows; where customers are having fun we can be sure that the Delight Factor is operating. On the other hand, the experience of delight need not always be accompanied by a feeling of fun. What follows in this section is a variety of nudges, some of which can engender more fun than others.

Games. Using games and competitions to stimulate involvement in the design, production, marketing and delivery of goods and services can nudge some customers into delight. Care, however, needs to be taken to avoid antagonising those customers whose sense of humour may not align with that of the service provider.

Help Desk. Easily accessible, low-cost advice services can nudge those customers whose problems can be readily solved over the phone. Care needs to be taken to avoid delays in the provision of help, such as being kept on 'hold' for more than a few minutes. The use of 'hold jockeys' who stay with the waiting customer, keeping him or her advised of progress, or using waiting time for giving general advice or playing music can with careful research and planning make the customer predisposed to being nudged. However, if the customer perceives the help desk as a problem reinforcer rather than a problem solver, the scope for nudging disappears.

Hosting. Providing corporate entertainment as a means of rewarding customer loyalty may act as a nudge. It can be, however, an expensive device which is interpreted as a bribe rather than a nudge. Furthermore, it can have an alienating effect on those loyal customers who do not benefit from the hospitality. Nudges need to have their source primarily in hearts and minds, and not solely in pockets.

Housekeeping. High standards of cleanliness and hygiene can act as nudges, particularly when applied to toilets, kitchens and behind the scenes which the customer may inadvertently visit.

Incentives. These may range from discounts and free-gifts to bonuses and prizes. The danger is that their existence can detract from the psychic aspects of service. Another danger is that dissatisfaction with the incentive can lead to reduced satisfaction with the core product or service to which it relates.

Information. The importance of providing customers with the information they want is often under-rated. Clear, timely and accurate information to the customer will often provide just the nudge required in moving from satisfaction to delight.

Innovation. This is usually thought of in terms of significant new products or services. While these are important, a nudge can often be the consequence of doing things a little bit differently and a tiny bit better than the competition.

Juggling. Used in a metaphorical sense, this refers to the ability to cope effectively with more than one activity or customer at the same time. All a nudge need take is pleasantly acknowledging the arrival of a customer while serving another. More elaborate juggling requires the consent of all customers involved if it is to be an effective nudge.

From Keenness to Niches

Managing the Delight Factor calls for the ability to do ordinary things in an extraordinary way. The next clutch of nudges may, like all those listed, appear as normal routines. This may well be the case, but the essence of 'nudging into delight' is to use the ordinary to bring about the extraordinary. A conductor's baton is simply a piece of wood; in one pair of hands it can help an orchestra make music, in another pair of hands it can enable the same orchestra to create magic.

Keenness. Displaying a spontaneous willingness to be helpful is always refreshing to customers and can often nudge them into delight.

Know-how. Keenness by itself will not always suffice. It needs to be accompanied by know-how if delight is to be sustained. Displaying ready mastery of a subject or situation can be a powerful nudge.

Logistics. The way in which goods are stored and distributed or services are laid out and presented can be a powerful nudge. The ability to supply 'out-of-stock' items swifter than the competition, care in the spacing of tables in restaurants, all seats having a full view of the stage in a theatre, and the proximity of toilets in public places are but a few examples of how attention to logistics can influence customers' perceptions. This nudge is particularly relevant for managing the Delight Factor for those customers with problems of mobility or confined to wheelchairs.

Loyalty. This is a two way process. Customer loyalty needs to be reciprocated. Those companies which help their established customers through difficult times have a much better chance of nudging than their counterparts who prove to be fair weather friends.

Manners. Courtesy is not a concept; it is a way of behaving which manifests itself in good manners. Displaying a code of conduct which is appropriate to the accepted practices of civilised behaviour can be the nudge that makes the difference.

Massaging. This is the art of making subtle adjustments to products and situations which increases the comfort level of the customer. By making a product or service more personalised the customer can be nudged into delight.

Memory. This is more than remembering names and faces. It is the ability to recall the customers' likes and dislikes, and to evoke memories of pleasant experiences. By such means the self-esteem of the customer will be raised and there will be a predisposition to be nudged into delight.

Merchandising. 'Laying one's stall out' to attract the customer is possibly the oldest example of invoking the Delight Factor. It still works.

Morality. In an age of default, where customers suffer from corporate misbehaviour, abiding by a code of values and beliefs which are congruent with the law and customs of society is an increasingly useful nudge, though difficult to publicise.

Niches. Finding niches within niches is essential to success in managing the Delight Factor. Armed with a comprehensive customer profile in terms of needs, expectations, values and lifestyle, it is easier to design a custom-made nudge than a rough tool.

From Observation to Zeal

This final clutch of nudges reinforces the view that when it comes to managing the Delight Factor, it is essential to have a well-tuned antenna which is capable of picking up signals of customer needs and expectations. The prize of competitive advantage goes to the company which can pick up weak signals at an early stage, using them to select the most appropriate nudge.

Observation. Keeping alert to the verbal and non-verbal messages given off by the customer enables the service provider to nudge on a broader front than would otherwise be the case.

Panache. Transforming the mundane into the exciting is a powerful nudge. By displaying a fresh and attractive approach to what hitherto has been routine, the service provider can become the delight provider.

Patience. Willingly taking more time than normal to help the customer achieve the desired goal can pay dividends in the form of repeat business. The main point in using this nudge is to appear not to rush the customer, even if the actual time taken is very short. This can be achieved by the careful use of 'no hurry' words and body language.

Piggy-backing. Combining a product or service with another at minimal cost can be an effective nudge. Examples are providing free magazines to hotel guests, and giving free samples of food or perfumes along with the standard product.

Privacy. Ensuring that the customer can conduct a transaction with the minimum of interruption is a useful nudge. This can be achieved by such means as not accepting telephone calls while dealing with the customer, or the provision of private areas or visiting the customer at home.

Question Handling. Listening and responding quickly to questions posed by customers is a relatively simple nudge which can easily be over-looked. The essential skill here is to listen, not only to the words, but to 'hidden' messages which the customer for some reason or other is hesitant to articulate.

Recognition. Everyone enjoys recognition. The use of names, acknowledgement of one's presence, and remembering previous encounters, all help to nudge a customer into delight.

Reliability. Keeping promises builds a reputation for dependability, which results in the customer being released from anxiety and apprehension and therefore in a positive emotional state which can make delight easier to achieve.

Respect. Treating the customer as an intelligent fellow human being enhances self-worth and makes nudging easier.

Responsiveness. Displaying the ability to anticipate or react to needs and expectations at a pace which is comfortable for the customer is an effective nudge.

Self-service. This can be a nudge – providing the customer prefers self-service and can do so without embarrassment. Faulty equipment, unclear instruction and other hazards must be swept away if this nudge is to work.

Standards. Providing explicit details of what the customer can expect, and sustaining the standards at the point of delivery will produce a powerful nudge.

Thoughtfulness. Displaying a greater degree of concern or helpfulness than the customer would normally expect will almost certainly act as a nudge. Little things such as a 'get well' card, or providing a cup of coffee while the customer is waiting can produce large effects.

User-friendly. Whether systems, products or procedures, those designed with the needs and capabilities of the customer in mind will be more effective at nudging than their company-biased counterparts.

Visibility. Customers put a higher premium on seeing managers and others responsible for servicing their needs than is often realised. A pleasant greeting from a manager can often be the trigger needed for nudging.

Warmth. Conveying a sense of spontaneous rapport can result in a favourable disposition in the customer, making it easier to nudge.

Zeal. Displaying an eagerness to care for the customer and leaving no stone unturned in the pursuit of solutions to the customer's problem is more than a nudge; it is the ideal way to transport the customer into the realm of delight.

Conclusion

Nudging is a skill which improves with practice. Nudge too forcibly and the customer will resist, nudge too weakly and the customer will be unmoved. The secret of successful nudging is to select the appropriate type of nudge and apply the degree of pressure which will result in the customer moving willingly into the realm of delight.

Drawing on some of the nudges described in this chapter, Table 7.1 makes a distinction between the state of satisfaction and that of delight. The difference between a satisfied customer and a delighted one requires little more than a nudge.

Most successful nudges have their roots in emotions and the senses. How, through these, it is possible to create a sense of delight is what we shall now explore.

TABLE 7.1

NUDGING CUSTOMERS FROM SATISFACTION TO DELIGHT

The Nudge	From Satisfaction	To Delight
Accessibility – ensuring customers can gain easy access to person/ service they want.	– Customer able to contact the right person with minimal involvement of intermediaries.	– Right person anticipates likely needs of customer and initiates contact at a convenient time.
	– When right person not available stand-in provides service.	– When right person not available, he/she forewarns stand-in of likelihood of customer calling. Alternatively, right person contacts customer prior to departure and forestalls need for subsequent customer contact.
	– Contact can be made during normal working hours.	– Contact can be made at any time.
Added Value – enhancement of the basic value of products/services.	– Provide little extras which exceed those offered by the competition.	– Seek what added value the customer would prefer and provide it in physical, psychological and/or spiritual terms.
		(cont'd...)

TABLE 7.1
NUDGING CUSTOMERS FROM SATISFACTION TO DELIGHT

The Nudge	From Satisfaction	To Delight
Added Value – enhancement of the basic value of products/services.	– Provide loyalty bonuses to regular customers.	– Ask regular customers what they would appreciate in terms of a loyalty bonus and, where feasible, provide it.
Advice – anticipating and seeking the nature of guidance which customer needs to resolve a problem.	– Provide solution which customer can apply successfully. – Check that problem has been resolved to customer's satisfaction.	– Take over problem from customer and resolve it. – Check that problem has been resolved to customer's delight.
Ambience – providing an environment which is conducive to the well-being of customers.	– Ensure that encounter area is clean and comfortable. – Creation of a climate of friendly efficiency.	– Ensure that encounter area enhances customer self-image. – Creation of a climate of genuine and spontaneous care.
Anniversaries – using commemorative events to reinforce the customer bond.	– Provide acceptable momento of an anniversary significant to the company.	– Provide acceptable momento of an anniversary significant to the customer who is happy to receive such recognition.

(cont'd...)

TABLE 7.1
NUDGING CUSTOMERS FROM SATISFACTION TO DELIGHT

The Nudge	From Satisfaction	To Delight
Anniversaries – using commemorative events to reinforce the customer bond.	– Provide commemoration of matter of national interest.	– Provide commemoration of a matter of local interest.
Appearance – the image perceived by the customer of the dress, personal presentation of the service provider.	– Dress, demeanour and physical appearance of staff adds to the pleasantness of the service encounter.	– Dress, demeanour and physical appearance of staff reinforces the self-esteem of the customer and results in a memorable service experience.
	– Uniforms are worn and create a good impression.	– Uniforms play a role which helps the customer to satisfy his/her needs with greater ease than would otherwise be the case.
Assurance – the ability to put at rest the fears and concerns of customers.	– Customers are dealt with in a caring and professional manner which addresses common fears and concerns.	– Individual fears and concerns are identified through sensitive probing and addressed in a personalised and truthful manner.
	– Customers are effectively helped to deal with their worries.	– Worries are taken away from customers and dealt with by the service provider.

(cont'd....)

TABLE 7.1
NUDGING CUSTOMERS FROM SATISFACTION TO DELIGHT

The Nudge	From Satisfaction	To Delight
Assurance – the ability to put at rest the fears and concerns of customers.	– Regular checking of customers' concerns and fears.	– Anticipation of customers' concerns and fears.
Behaviour – everything we do and everything we say.	– Behaviour of service provider is marked by friendliness and a willingness to help. – Behaviour is recognised as being central to others perception of us and is used appropriately.	– Behaviour of service provider results in a symbiosis of enhanced self-esteem for both parties. – Behaviour is recognised as being the primary resource for trans-forming situations and transcending perceived limitations to human potential.
Bonding – the ability to retain customer loyalty against competing pressures.	– Regular customers perceive that they receive some form of special treatment. – Continuous customership is ack-nowledged in some tangible way.	– Regular customers have clearly defined entitlements, particularly in emergency situations. – Customers are courted in a discreet manner which reinforces their self-esteem.

(cont'd...)

TABLE 7.1
NUDGING CUSTOMERS FROM SATISFACTION TO DELIGHT

The Nudge	From Satisfaction	To Delight
Care – the presence of attitudes and behaviours which create a perception of genuine concern for the total well-being of the customer.	– Experience of care in the manner in which one receives service which meets a need.	– A holistic approach to well-being which transcends the service need and encompasses care for the environment and the rights of all affected by company action.
Codes – statements of action which are undertaken to ensure specified standards of service.	– Code is clearly defined and exceeds legislative requirements. – Code defines standard service and providers seek to abide by it.	– Code is the result of collaborative effort by customers and the service provider. – Code defines minimal service and providers are expected to exceed it.
Communications – the process of conveying information in a manner which is fully understood by the recipient.	– All types of information are conveyed clearly and at the right time.	– Communications is recognised as incorporating body language and this is taken into account whenever information is conveyed. – The effective management of communications is accepted as a critical task which is on-going.

(cont'd....)

TABLE 7.1

NUDGING CUSTOMERS FROM SATISFACTION TO DELIGHT

The Nudge	*From Satisfaction*	*To Delight*
Communications – the process of conveying information in a manner which is fully understood by the recipient.		– The selection of the appropriate media receives as much attention as the construction of the message.
Competence – the display of mastery of a subject by selecting and applying the appropriate blend of knowledge and skill in resolving a problem.	– Service providers are well trained to respond to customers' needs and expectations.	– Service providers are well trained to be pro-active by anticipating customers' needs and meeting them in a manner which habitually exceeds expectations.
	– Professionalism is evident at all service levels in the company's care activities.	– Professionalism is evident in all activities undertaken by the company or on its behalf by agents.
Complaints Handling – the process of receiving and responding to claims by customers that products/services do not meet prescribed standards.	– There is an efficient, hassle-free complaints handling procedure.	– Every employee can handle complaints and resolve them in most cases on the spot.

(cont'd...)

TABLE 7.1
NUDGING CUSTOMERS FROM SATISFACTION TO DELIGHT

The Nudge	From Satisfaction	To Delight
Complaints Handling – the process of receiving and responding to claims by customers that products/services do not meet prescribed standards.	– Complaints are identified as guides to improving performance/products. – Complaints are well received.	– Complaints are genuinely welcomed as opportunities to enhance the reputation of the company in respect of product/service quality. – Complaints are sought.
Confidentiality – the safeguarding of customer data, within the limits of legal requirements.	– There are clearly defined procedures and physical safeguards for ensuring security of data.	– There is clear evidence that staff are concerned to safeguard confidentiality in a manner which is sensitive to the feelings and rights of all involved.
	– The privacy of customers is respected within the constraints of the lay-out of the building.	– Ensuring customer's privacy, where appropriate, is a prime requirement in the design and lay-out of buildings and the training of staff.
Courtesy – interacting with customers in a manner which dignifies the relationship.	– Staff speak and behave in a manner which is consistent with high and acceptable standards of social behaviour.	– Care is taken to enhance the self-esteem of customers in subtle ways which are perceived to be genuine. (cont'd....)

TABLE 7.1

NUDGING CUSTOMERS FROM SATISFACTION TO DELIGHT

The Nudge	From Satisfaction	To Delight
Courtesy – interacting with customers in a manner which dignifies the relationship.	– Symbols of courtesy such a polite-ness and use of appropriate nomenclature are evident at all levels.	– There is evidence of a culture of courtesy which permeates all relationships and is sustained in all circumstances.
Credibility – the extent to which the judgement and the advice of the service provider is trusted by the customer.	– There is a tradition of under-promising and over delivering.	– Customer is made to feel that his/her views are important in providing the desired outcomes of decisions.
	– Claims on matters of reliability, durability, consequences are substantiated.	– Customer is happy to vouch for credibility of the service provider.
Cycles of Service – the process involved from identifying a customer's need to its satisfaction.	– Cycles are at a pace consistent with the needs and circumstances of most customers.	– Cycles are personalised.
	– Attention is paid to improving the speed and/or smoothness of each cycle.	– Attention is focused on eliminating non-essential cycles without jeopardising customer care.

(cont'd....)

TABLE 7.1
NUDGING CUSTOMERS FROM SATISFACTION TO DELIGHT

The Nudge	From Satisfaction	To Delight
Delivery – the provision of the required product/service to the customer.	– Delivery is on time as specified by the company and conforms to customer's requirements.	– Delivery is at the time most convenient for the customer.
	– The manner of delivery shows care and concern.	– The manner of delivery adds value to the product/ service, in a way most acceptable to the customer.
Diversions – activities which add to the enjoyment of a customer at times of difficulty in a service encounter, e.g., long queues.	– Diversion distracts customer from potential cause of dissatisfaction.	– Diversion adds value to the service encounter.
Empathy – the ability to project oneself into the mind-set of others, leading to a full understanding of their perceptions and needs.	– Service provider treats customer as provider would want to be treated.	– Service provider treats customer as customer wants to be treated.

(cont'd....)

TABLE 7.1

NUDGING CUSTOMERS FROM SATISFACTION TO DELIGHT

The Nudge	From Satisfaction	To Delight
Empathy – the ability to project one-self into the mind-set of others, leading to a full understanding of their perceptions and needs.	– Service provider responds to customer's need in a way which takes account of the context of the situation in which the customer is placed.	– Service provider finds ways of changing the context of the situation if this would be welcomed by the customer, e.g., moves location of service encounter from office to home.
Endurance – the capacity to tolerate difficult customers and/or situations.	– Consistently pleasant behaviour at all times. – Maintain high levels of stamina despite varying pressures.	– Identify cause of annoyance or difficulty and remove it as quickly as possible. – Structure work-load to control level of pressure on service providers.
Enthusiasm – the ability to sustain feelings of zest for meeting the needs of customers.	– There is a range of activities to ensure the maintenance of customer orientation. – There is a variety of awards and other recognition devices for special performance.	– All staff are made to feel that customer service lies at the core of any business. – All staff are made to feel that their contribution to service quality is valuable.

(cont'd....)

TABLE 7.1

NUDGING CUSTOMERS FROM SATISFACTION TO DELIGHT

The Nudge	From Satisfaction	To Delight
Fairness – conveying to customers that they are being treated in an even-handed way.	– Customer can receive compensation if product/service does not meet specified criteria. – Customers are made aware of small print before committing themselves.	– Customer is aware that compensation will apply to psychic as well as physical damage. – No small print.
Feedback – the eliciting, analysis of and acting on customers' reactions to a product or event.	– Market research is carried out regularly and acted on to raise the level of customer satisfaction.	– Market research is an on-going activity by all staff.
Flexibility – the ease with which policies and procedures can be adjusted to meet the special needs of customers.	– There is a clear guidance of staff on the extent to which rules can be bent. – A small charge may be made for changes to meet special needs.	– Staff are empowered to meet the special needs of customers by using their discretion. – No charges are made for small changes to meet special needs.
Follow-through – the process of ensuring that commitments made to customers are met.	– There are clearly defined procedures for ensuring that commitments are met.	– Customers are kept informed of progress in fulfilling commitments.

(cont'd....)

TABLE 7.1
NUDGING CUSTOMERS FROM SATISFACTION TO DELIGHT

The Nudge	From Satisfaction	To Delight
Follow-through – the process of ensuring that commitments made to customers are met.	– There is forewarning to customers of any undue delay in meeting commitments.	– There is a culture of continuous care and commitment to deadlines.
Goodwill – the capacity to generate feelings of enjoyment among customers.	– Various events are held, e.g., open days, to entertain customers. – Presents are provided to customers as a token of appreciation.	– Customers experience good feelings whenever in contact with the company. – Boosting self-worth of customers is accepted as the best way of generating goodwill.
Helpfulness – the capacity to provide the level of support and/or guidance appropriate to customers' needs.	– Help desk exists and is easily accessible. – Clearly written help aids are readily available.	– All customer contact staff are of direct help in virtually all situations. – Help is given in a manner which personalises it.
Innovation – the ability to find new and improved ways of meeting customers' needs.	– Novel approaches to meeting customer needs are encouraged.	– A sense of customer-oriented creativity pervades the organisation and innovation influences all activities.

(cont'd...)

TABLE 7.1
NUDGING CUSTOMERS FROM SATISFACTION TO DELIGHT

The Nudge	From Satisfaction	To Delight
Innovation – the ability to find new and improved ways of meeting customers' needs.	– A staff suggestion scheme exists.	– Customers and suppliers are encouraged to suggest innovations.
Judgement – the ability to evaluate the key factors in a situation and take action appropriate to the needs of the customer.	– When in doubt judgements are made in favour of the customer. – Reasons for reaching conclusions are available to customers.	– Judgements are always made in favour of the customer within legal and financial constraints. – Customers are forewarned of likely judgements and are helped to cope with consequences.
Know-how – the capacity to have readily available the knowledge and skills required to meet customers' needs.	– Staff are kept up-dated on necessary knowledge and skills. – There is in operation a system defining 'who knows what'.	– There are arrangements for anticipating changes in knowledge and skills. – Staff are capable of performing a variety of roles.
Leadership – the ability to inspire in others a ready willingness to achieve goals set by the leader.	– Leader is recognised as being customer oriented.	– All staff are customer oriented, whether or not the leader is present.

(cont'd...)

TABLE 7.1
NUDGING CUSTOMERS FROM SATISFACTION TO DELIGHT

The Nudge	From Satisfaction	To Delight
Leadership – the ability to inspire in others a ready willingness to achieve goals set by the leader.	– Leader is highly visible to customers.	– Leader is readily accessible to customers.
Motivation – the process through which staff are encouraged to provide high levels of customer care.	– Financial reward system is geared to the provision of high quality customer care. – There are special events to reinforce staff motivation.	– Staff receive psychic up-lift in providing customer care. – Customer care is intrinsic to all activities and all staff are imbued with it in their motivational make-up.
Needs Analysis – the process for determining what customers are seeking from the company.	– Regular surveys of product/service preferences of customers. – Customers' views sought and used in up-dating products/services.	– On-going analysis of psychological and spiritual, as well as physical desires of customers. – Customers' views dominate in all developments of products/services.
Options – the process of providing customers with alternative ways of satisfying their needs.	– Customers are given choices.	– Customers are asked what choices they wish to have. (cont'd…)

— 155 —

TABLE 7.1
NUDGING CUSTOMERS FROM SATISFACTION TO DELIGHT

The Nudge	From Satisfaction	To Delight
Options – the process of providing customers with alternative ways of satisfying their needs.	– Guidance is given in weighing up the pros and cons of alternatives.	– Customers are advised to select option which is in their best interest.
Perceptions – the cluster of emotions and senses which combine to determine the customer's view of a situation and his/her resulting behaviour.	– Positive perceptions are the result of specific policies and procedures.	– Positive perceptions are the result of repeated good experiences.
	– Negative perceptions are worked on once they are brought to attention of company.	– Causes of negative perceptions are anticipated and acted on before they have a chance to influence the customer.
Recognition – the capacity to acknowledge the presence, self-worth and needs of customers.	– Service providers acknowledge presence of customer rapidly and attend to their needs as swiftly as possible.	– Service provider gives the customer the form of recognition with which the latter is most comfortable.
	– A spirit of friendliness pervades the company and is reflected in the manner of contact.	– A spirit of helpfulness pervades the company. Customers do not have to seek out the service provider.

(cont'd...)

TABLE 7.1
NUDGING CUSTOMERS FROM SATISFACTION TO DELIGHT

The Nudge	From Satisfaction	To Delight
Reliability – the process of consistent conformance to specified standards.	– There is a zero-faults product policy. – Any fault is swiftly remedied.	– Reliability extends to all aspects of the company. – All faults are perceived as improvement opportunities.
Security – the process of safeguarding the customer and his/her belongings while being dealt with by the service provider.	– There are clearly defined safety drills, adequate guards and reliable alarm systems.	– Security is of the highest order but is discreet and non-threatening.
Standards – clearly defined specification of performance to be delivered to the customer.	– There are clearly defined standards and measures for key areas of performance. – Standards and measures are reviewed from time-to-time.	– Standards are treated as minimal levels of performance. – Standards and measures are regularly adjusted to meet anticipated customer needs.

Chapter 8

Creating a Sense of Delight

Introduction

Delight is experienced in two ways: physically through the senses, and psychologically through the emotions. Often the sensual and the emotional are intertwined, making it difficult to identify which is the dominant force shaping the experience. However, if the experience is to be managed it is necessary to unravel the intertwining elements in order to identify optimum ways of interlinking them in order to strengthen the Delight Factor.

In this chapter we will begin by analysing the role of the senses, then move on to the emotions. In both cases the aim is to eliminate the 'Delight Killers' listed in Table 8.1.

Delighting the Senses

All five senses – hearing, sight, smell, taste and touch – make individual and joint contributions to the Delight Factor. These contributions are summarised in Table 8.2.

Hearing

Hearing is the capacity to receive, analyse, identify and give meaning to different sounds using the ear. It is this sense which enables us to enjoy the conversation of others, be enraptured by music, be alerted to the passage of time, and be forewarned of danger.

Sound can help or hinder the Delight Factor in a variety of ways:

TABLE 8.1
THE DELIGHT KILLERS IN CUSTOMER CARE

Behavioural Killers

Banality	– talking only at a superficial level and being repetitious when the customer is seeking a meaningful conversation.
Ingratiating	– trying unsuccessfully to be funny; seeking to be over-whelmingly nice.
Negativism	– always looking on the depressing side of things; continuously complaining.
Over-seriousness	– rarely smiling; using a serious tone of voice even when trying to be light-hearted and amusing.
Passivity	– unwilling to express opinions.
Self-preoccupation	– showing little interest in the customer; talking mainly about self.
Tediousness	– talking too slowly; taking too long to reply; extending conversation beyond its normal length.
Unenthusiastic	– avoiding eye contact; lacking expressiveness; talking in a monotone.

Sense Killers

Bad smells.
Loud noise.
Inadequate lighting.
Lighting too powerful.
Garish decor.
Lack of maintenance.
Chipped crockery.
Broken equipment.
Temperature too high or too low.
Lack of signs.
Unhygienic practices.
Lack of cleanliness.

Emotional Killers

Angry responses to customer's requests.
Expressing contempt for the customer.
Heightening anxiety unnecessarily.
Showing disgust at customer's choice.
Being impatient with the customer.
Lacking empathy.
Ignoring the customer.

TABLE 8.2
CREATING A SENSE OF DELIGHT

Sense	Delight Factor Opportunities	Examples
Hearing – the capacity to receive, analyse, identify and give meaning to different sounds by use of the ear.	– Reinforce the emotions that delight.	– Use of music to increase emotional impact of an event, e.g., an anniversary.
	– Reinforce a feeling of total involvement in a situation.	– Eliminate noise so that customer can concentrate on enjoying an event.
	– Save time of customer.	– Effective listening eliminates need for repetition and delays due to miscommunication.
	– Boost self-worth of customer.	– Effective listening creates perception that customer is 'someone worth listening to'.
	– Signal the beginning of a pleasurable event.	– Wedding bells.
	– Enhance the significance of an occasion.	– Music at an awards ceremony.
	– Provide reassurance, enabling customer to enjoy an event without worrying that a signal will sound if there is danger.	– Use of distinctive sounds to provide alarms and all clear.

(cont'd...)

TABLE 8.2
CREATING A SENSE OF DELIGHT

Sense	Delight Factor Opportunities	Examples
Hearing (cont'd)	– Contribute to the creation of appropriate mood.	– Soft music for romantic setting, etc.
	– Compensate for sight deficiencies of customers.	– Use of sounds which are commonly associated with certain events.
	– Compensate for hearing deficiencies of customers.	– Use of volume and pace of speech appropriate to age/hearing ability of customer.
	– Reinforce realism in simulated situations.	– Use of recorded sounds to reinforce visual impact of an event.
	– Evoke pleasant memories.	– Use of sounds which will result in nostalgia.
	– Reinforce the emotions that delight.	– Use of colour to increase emotional impact of an event, e.g., white or pastel shades at a wedding.
	– Reinforce a feeling of total involvement in a situation.	– Screen off all distracting sights.
Sight – the capacity to receive, analyse and identify different images by using the eye.	– Save customer's time.	– Provide clear and well situated signs.
		(cont'd...)

TABLE 8.2
CREATING A SENSE OF DELIGHT

Sense	Delight Factor Opportunities	Examples
Sight (cont'd)	– Create a feeling of surprise.	– Keep surprise well hidden until the planned moment of impact.
	– Stimulate positive expectations.	– Reveal images at a measured pace which results in mounting excitement.
	– Reinforce a focal point.	– Draw attention to a specific object which will shape desired perception.
	– Reinforce customer's self-worth.	– Restrict 'viewing' to a selected clientele.
	– Create diversion for the customer.	– Draw attention away from undesired image by showing more attractive alternative.
	– Enhance attractiveness of an object or situation.	– Use lighting and other devices to improve visual impact.
	– Using packaging that increases psychic value added – (but avoid overpackaging).	– Package not only attracts, but is integral part of total appeal of product, e.g., perfume bottle.
		(cont'd...)

**TABLE 8.2
CREATING A SENSE OF DELIGHT**

Sense	Delight Factor Opportunities	Examples
Sight (cont'd)	– Convey a feeling of pride in appearance.	– All premises to be in a pristine state of decoration and repair; staff to be well-groomed.
	– Contribute to the creation of appropriate mood.	– Subdued lighting for romance; bright colours for keep-fit exercises.
	– Compensate for hearing deficiencies of customers.	– Use of visual aids to convey messages.
	– Reinforce realism in simulated situations.	– Use of 'artificial' flowers.
	– Stimulate appetite.	– Attractive colouring and display of food and drink.
	– Provide signals to avoid danger.	– Red for 'stop'; green for 'go'.
	– Evoke pleasant memories.	– Use images which will result in pleasurable nostalgia.
	– Enhance customer's self-image.	– Guide customer in use of appropriate colours in all aspects of their appearance.

(cont'd...)

TABLE 8.2
CREATING A SENSE OF DELIGHT

Sense	Delight Factor Opportunities	Examples
Sight (cont'd)	– Reinforce customer loyalty.	– Use distinctive colour for 'branding', easing identification by customer.
	– Compensate for sight deficiencies in customers.	– Use of large print for the elderly.
	– Prevent mishaps in the dark.	– Use of luminous devices.
	– Overcome language barriers.	– Internationally agreed symbols and colour combinations on signs, instructions.
	– Differentiate economic values of items.	– Different colours of currency notes; use of 'gold', 'silver', 'bronze' to distinguish service levels.
	– Reinforce the emotions that delight.	– Use of floral perfumes, incense, and pleasant odours associated with emotional events such as marriage.
Smell – the capacity to receive, analyse, identify and react to the odours of different substances using the nose.	– Reinforce a feeling of total involvement in a situation.	– Avoid the intrusion of unpleasant or inappropriate odours.

(cont'd...)

TABLE 8.2
CREATING A SENSE OF DELIGHT

Sense	Delight Factor Opportunities	Examples
Smell (cont'd)	– Save customer's time.	– Reduce frequency of washing self or clothes by use of substances which convey a 'clean smell'.
	– Boost customer's self-worth.	– Provide guidance on use of perfumes which are associated with customers' idealised self-image.
	– Heighten appeal of products.	– Product impregnated with rein-forced natural smell.
	– Convey a feeling of pride in appearance.	– Advise customer on perfume appropriate to their skin type.
	– Contribute to the creation of appropriate mood.	– Use of sexually arousing smells to create a romantic mood.
	– Reinforce achievement of desired goal.	– Use in cleansers of smells associated with 'cleanliness' in a particular culture.
	– Compensate for sight deficiencies in customers.	– Use of scents to create or rein-force an image of a product, e.g., a freshly baked loaf.
		(cont'd...)

TABLE 8.2
CREATING A SENSE OF DELIGHT

Sense	Delight Factor Opportunities	Examples
Smell (cont'd)	– Reinforce realism in simulated situations.	– Use of 'jungle' smells in a 'tropical jungle' attraction in a theme park.
	– Stimulate appetite.	– Releasing food smells prior to serving a meal.
	– Evoke pleasant memories.	– Use smell which will result in nostalgia.
	– Reinforce attractiveness of a product.	– Product image and smell are congruent – a simulated leather product smells like leather, not plastic.
	– Eliminate obnoxious smells.	– Provide physical and/or chemical devices for eliminating or covering obnoxious smells.
	– Personalise products.	– Letters impregnated with writer's special perfume.
	– Reinforce special nature of an occasion.	– Use of products exhuding smells associated with Christmas.
		(cont'd...)

TABLE 8.2
CREATING A SENSE OF DELIGHT

Sense	Delight Factor Opportunities	Examples
Smell (cont'd)	– Transform the potentially embarrassing. – Provide reassurance. – Stimulate desire in advertising. – Increase tangibility of the intangible. – Make the undesirable more desirable.	– Pleasantly perfumed ointments and other externally used medicines. – Product 'smells right'. – Use of 'scratch and sniff' advertisement. – Create scents which will be associated with such concepts as 'achievement'. – Create attractive smells for ugly food such as some fish, and also for odourless synthetic food.
Taste – the capacity to receive, analyse and identify different flavours and textures of edible substances using the mouth.	– Reinforce the emotions that delight. – Create surprise.	– Provision of 'fun' foods, e.g. 'cheese chocolates'. – Taste and/or sensation of eating food is a pleasant surprise due to novelty or manner of presentation. (cont'd...)

TABLE 8.2
CREATING A SENSE OF DELIGHT

Sense	Delight Factor Opportunities	Examples
Taste (cont'd)	– Extend options for enjoying preferred flavours.	– 'Ice-cream' tasting like fruit or other confectionery.
	– Save time of customer.	– Reduce eating time by making food possible to drink rather than eat.
	– Reinforce customer's self-worth.	– Convey care in the selection, preparation, cooking and serving of food 'just for you'.
	– Contribute to the creation of appropriate mood.	– Provide food and drink associated with romance, luxury, etc.
	– Evoke memories.	– Provide food and drink which will result in pleasurable nostalgia.
	– Reinforce sense of occasion.	– Provide food and drink traditionally associated with special occasions.
	– Contribute to feeling of well-being.	– Provide nutritious food in health promoting ways.
	– Tighten bond with customer.	– Share or provide meal as an appreciation of past custom.
		(cont'd...)

TABLE 8.2
CREATING A SENSE OF DELIGHT

Sense	Delight Factor Opportunities	Examples
Taste (cont'd)	– Enhance customer's self-image. – Provide for customer's special dietary needs. – Provide food that customer wants when he/she wants it.	– Provide clear guidance on the correct manner for eating 'unusual' food. – Cater for babies, the elderly, vegetarians, etc. – All-day breakfasts.
Touch – the capacity to receive, analyse, identify and react to pressures and other sensations affecting the skin.	– Reinforce the emotions that delight. – Ensure that surfaces feel clean. – Furniture and equipment which are comfortable as well as functional. – Temperature levels which are comfortable. – Containers which are easy to open. – Equipment which is simple to operate.	– The feel of clothes that fit well, a friendly hand-shake. – Well-polished non-slip floors. – Chairs which are ergonomically designed. – Efficient air-conditioning. – Bottles and cans which do not pose problems for elderly customers. – Remote-control mechanisms which are reliable and 'feel good'.

- Direct speech.
- Noise.
- Use of audio equipment.
- Enhancing privacy.
- Creating and reinforcing moods.
- Evoking memories.

In the service encounter, most communication will be by the spoken word. The tone, pitch and speed of speaking greatly affects the customer's perceptions. While it need not be essential for service providers to receive elocution lessons, they should be made aware of the impact of their voice on customers. Habits such as drawling, droning, spluttering and whispering are unlikely to create a sense of delight. On the other hand, speaking clearly, with a feeling of warmth and at a pace suitable to the listener will make the customer more disposed to a sense of delight.

Noise is unwanted sound; one person's noise is another person's music. In service encounters, noises such as the banging of doors, the clatter of cutlery, and the hum of machinery can all create distractions and reduce the satisfaction level of the customer. Where possible, steps should be taken to remove the cause of the noise, or use noise reduction measures such as 'white noise'. This operates by broadcasting sound across a wide range of frequencies, resulting in an electronic blocking out of noise.

Few sounds are more disturbing to customers than the cacophony produced by malfunctioning or inappropriately used public address systems. Otherwise excellent service on an aircraft can be spoiled by inaudible or over-loud messages emanating from the cockpit or galley. Passengers at stations become enraged when all that they are able to make out from an announcement is the name of their desired destination. Clear, concise, informative and timely announcements can make the difference between delight and despair on the part of customers. The Delight Factor depends on competent use of reliable equipment in all activities, particularly those intended to provide vital information.

The use of sound to facilitate privacy is important where customers have to hold private conversations in open places, such as banks, medical reception areas, or restaurants. The important point to keep in mind is that the volume and pace of background music should provide privacy without intrusion. A similar point can be made about 'mood music', the aim here is that the music should be an integral part of the service experience. It must therefore be congruent with the main activity.

Sight

Vision provides us with the capacity to receive, analyse and identify different images using our eyes. It is through our eyes that we are delighted or repelled by images of customer care. As with the other senses, sight acts on its own and also reinforces the messages we receive through other senses. Sights can distract, so in managing the Delight Factor it is important to set the scene in ways which will cause the customer to focus and not let eyes wander. Eye contact is essential for conveying warmth, concern and interest, but staring must be avoided since it can raise anxiety and cause discomfort.

In seeking to evoke delight the one thing that any service provider can do is smile. The sight of a broad, genuine smile can transform a situation. Ideally, both parties should smile spontaneously, but a social smile on the face of the service provider can work wonders. Spontaneous smiling requires the use of two sets of muscles around the mouth and the eyes. Those round the mouth contract pulling up the corners of the lips, but those round the eyes cannot be consciously controlled; they only come into play when the smile is spontaneous.

Smiles are infectious and can alter moods. This is due to a nerve connection between the facial muscles and the hypothalamus, the part of the brain which controls the emotions.

In any service encounter the provider can influence the mood of the customer by smiling; this sends a social signal that the provider is pleased to be of service, thus enhancing the self-esteem of the customer. The sight of a smile can be the nudge which shifts the customer from satisfaction to delight.

Smell

The sense of smell provides us with the capacity to receive, analyse, identify and react to the odours of different substances by the use of the nose. It is the most direct of all the senses. We can plug our ears, close our eyes, shut our mouths, and hold back from touching, but it is almost impossible to keep smells away from our nasal membranes. Each of us carries around aromatic memories which are triggered by recurrences of smells of the past.

In terms of using smells to stimulate delight, it is important to bear in mind the seven categories of smell which most people experience almost daily:

- Acrid – sharp smells associated with vinegar and bitter-tasting substances.
- Ethereal – delicate, short lasting smell of fresh fruits such as strawberries.
- Floral – delicate short lasting smell of flowers such as roses.
- Foul – strong stench of bad eggs, dirty drains.
- Minty – strong smell of peppermint.
- Musky – relatively strong but pleasant smell associated with many perfumes and cosmetics.
- Resinous – a strong but pleasant smell associated with pine, camphor and trees.

Smells can be transformed from the repulsive to the entrancing by dilution masking. In service companies there is an increasing tendency to simulate smells that delight. 'New car smell' sprays are wafted by used car dealers to create in the nose (and mind) of the customer a sense of buying a new car, even if it is several years old. Estate agents use 'cake baking' and 'new bread' aromas to entice potential house buyers to acquire an ideal home. There is a growing trend in shopping malls to discharge through the air conditioning a faint smell of pizza or other fast foods which are readily available.

Care needs to be taken in appealing to the sense of smell since preferences vary between nationalities, for example, in their household products Germans like resinous smells, particularly pine; the French prefer floral ones; and the Japanese go for the ethereal. North Americans prefer strong minty and resinous smells, but not so strong as the South Americans. In Venezuela, for instance, floor cleaning products contain ten times as much pine fragrance as those sold in the United States.

Although smells can create a sense of delight, the absence of foul smells can be as potent as the presence of fragrant ones.

Taste

Turning to the sense of taste, we know that much of the taste of food depends upon its smell. Taste is our capacity to receive, analyse and identify different flavours and textures of edible substances using the mouth. In relation to the Delight Factor, taste allows us to savour new gustatory experiences ranging from the highly palatable to the inedible.

Despite the immense variety of food and drink around the world, they all fit into four flavours:

- Sweet.
- Sour.
- Salt.
- Bitter.

Our taste buds are exceedingly small. We taste sweet things at the tip of our tongue; bitter things at the back; and sour and salty things at the side.

Varying taste combinations is one way of causing delight, but appealing to our gustatory memories can be even more potent. The phrases 'home made' and 'just like mother made it' evoke both a sensory and emotional response in customers. Although the reality may well be 'better than home made' or 'better than mother ever made it', no provider of food is willing to use such slogans and risk losing the Delight Factor.

Touch

Finally, we come to touch – our capacity to receive, analyse, identify and react to pressures and other sensations affecting the skin. In service encounters we experience touch in relation both to persons and things. Our hands can be the messengers of delight or its strangler. A firm but gentle handshake can put the customer at ease; a fumbled one can cause discomfort and embarrassment.

As with taste, inter-personal touching varies between nationalities and individuals. The service provider needs to be sensitive to the touch preferences of the customer. After an introductory handshake, the provider should leave it to the customer to give the lead in subsequent contact prior to a handshake on departure.

When it comes to touching objects, it is vital that surfaces feel clean and temperature levels are comfortable, that chairs are easy to rise from, and equipment is simple to operate. Some of the major contributions which technology can make to engendering delight through touch are:

- Containers which are both tamper proof and easy to open.
- Electronic equipment which is comfortably sited and simple to operate.
- Travelators and other mobility aids which are reliable and well paced.
- Equipment used only periodically which can be dismantled and is easy to store.

Touch can provide a physical feeling of delight, but just as important is the psychological feeling which has its source in the emotions. The difference between a kiss and sexual assault on the mouth is more a matter of emotion than physical contact.

Delighting the Emotions

Throughout the world it is becoming increasingly accepted that we can show feelings more freely than our predecessors did Three major factors have brought about the spread of greater tolerance for emotional displays:

- New patterns of parenting.
- The televising of actual events.
- The youth culture of the 1960s.

Child psychologists and popular writers on baby-care in the 1950s began to advocate the importance of the emotions in the development of the person. Doctor Benjamin Spock in his *Baby And Child Care* (The Bodley Head, British edition, 1955) dealt with the subject in a low-key way. But as the years have passed, the tantrum tolerance threshold has been raised. Fear of being accused of repressiveness changed the dictum 'children should be seen but not heard' to 'children must be heard as well as seen'. In effect, children have in Western societies been given increasing social permission to express negative as well as positive emotions publicly.

As the children of the 1950s passed through the mid-1960s and into the 1970s, emotional free expression was bolstered by rock concerts, protest marches, and the growing respectability of soft drugs. These emotional release events were televised. Adding to the emotional over-load of United States viewers was the total exposure of the Vietnam War. Scenes of horror were accompanied by open displays of fear, anger, and grief, not only at the battle front, but in cities scarred by terrorists outrages. Such horrific events were not confined to Vietnam. From Belfast to Beirut, from Paris to Peking, came, and continue to come, reflections of people like ourselves pouring out emotions to a global audience – the members of which feel empowered to release their emotional reservoir in public situations.

These influences flow over into the arena of customer care. The days of the reticent customer have been replaced by an era of assertiveness. The traditional view of man as 'the thinker' is giving way to man, 'the feeler'. The power of emotions in influencing consumer preferences is leading providers of products and services to seek out the ways in which they can use 'the emotional edge' as a competitive weapon.

Research suggests that a tiny almond shaped region deep in the temporal lobe of the brain masterminds our emotional response to situations. Known as the *amygdala,* and about the size of a fingernail, this region is believed to make the initial assessment of the emotional significance of any experience. In the case of basic emotions such as fear, the assessment and its associated initial response occur very swiftly.

There is growing scientific evidence that the brain is designed to react more to some things – a loud bang, for example – than to others. There appears to be an in-built alarm system which has been 'programmed' to make us wary of certain situations. It is this distinctive programme which can lead some people to exhibit phobias about spiders and snakes, while others have no problem in handling such creatures.

Just as the left and right hemispheres of the brain play different roles in our cognitive responses, so too do they exert complementary influences on our emotional responses. Experiments at the University of Wisconsin and the University of Oregon reveal that emotions such as fear and disgust are controlled, so to speak, by the right hemisphere, whereas sadness and happiness are governed by the left side.

As humankind has evolved over the millennia it has developed a repertoire of positive and negative emotions. The positive emotions drive people towards, or deeper into, situations which are pleasant and joyful; they encourage openness and a disposition to share the enjoyment. On the other side, negative emotions draw people away from situations which are perceived as threatening or hostile. This emotional armoury is designed to ensure the survival of the human species at a primitive level, but it is also carried into the battle of the market place as customers seek out those who supply delight, and shun those whose prices in terms of negative emotions are higher than we are willing to pay.

In terms of the Delight Factor there are three emotional states which are crucial:

- Anxiety.
- Embarrassment.
- Happiness.

Each of these has to be managed by the provider of products and services.

Banishing Anxiety

Anxiety, in the general, non-clinical sense, comes in several guises. Each of them produces a negative state of mind which must be displaced if delight is to take hold. The most common anxiety of customers is that caused by persistent doubts about the advisability of their choice of purchase. This niggling state of mind can be managed by communication, demonstration and restoration.

Communication, in particular the skillful use of questions, can remove this type of anxiety. Establishing the essential needs and expectations of the customer and being able to overcome them in an honest way can clear the mind of doubt.

Demonstration can be a more powerful slayer of nagging doubts since it impacts on more senses. The efficacy of a demonstration is vastly increased if the customer is able to conduct it. When it comes to assessing the merits of a product, the old adage 'seeing is believing' needs to share the platform of credibility with feeling, touching, hearing, tasting and smelling.

While direct experience of using a product is relatively easy to demonstrate, this is less so with a service. In this case, reference to third parties who have experience of the service can effectively substitute for the hands on experience of a physical demonstration. Another approach, but usually more expensive than referrals, is a 'trial run'. This can be provided free or at a discount. The difficulty with a 'trial run' is that the actual experience cannot be totally savoured since there is a time displacement at work. There will be subtle differences in ambience and in the disposition of the protagonists. This may raise the expectations of the customer when the 'real' experience occurs, resulting in a reduced level of satisfaction and a reinforcement of niggling worries.

Restoration, in the form of 'no quibble guarantees', is the most powerful weapon for combating anxiety. It removes the risk factor from the purchase decision, but it can be expensive. Once again, a no quibble guarantee is easier to apply to the tangible than to the intangible. Even in the former case, 'no quibble' has to be defined. Where a product fails to function because of deliberate abuse or wilful negligence, it is legitimate for the vendor to quibble.

Killing Embarrassment

At some stage or other every human being feels humiliated, diffident, awkward or ashamed. These feelings can be labelled together as the emotional state called 'embarrassment'.

Embarrassment can arise in many ways:

- Subjecting an individual to humiliation and mortification through a cruel premeditated act.
- Deflating an individual in a humbling or degrading way by some sort of 'put-down'.

- Catching someone wrong-footed by a surprise move which puts the person in an awkward position.
- Discomforting someone by showing annoyance or disdain.

Whatever form it takes, embarrassment is the antithesis of delight. Saving someone from embarrassment can, on the other hand, be a short-cut to delight. This is why emotional support for customers is so essential in managing the Delight Factor.

Situations which are routine for the service provider, such as flying, performing a medical operation, or finalising financial arrangements, can be stressful for the customer. Stress is a barrier to delight; embarrassment is a common cause of stress.

Emotional support can reduce or even eliminate stress, leaving the way open for the Delight Factor. Guidance on providing customers with emotional support not only in the case of embarrassment, but for other negative emotional states is given in Table 8.3. Emotions are listed alphabetically along with details of indicators of each emotion and examples of support mechanisms.

Creating Happiness

Like anxiety and embarrassment, happiness exists in many forms which fall into two categories:

- Long-lasting contentment.
- Short-term delight.

Long-lasting contentment produced on the basis of the Aristotelian concept of *eudomonia* – leading a rational and active life is what most of us seek. The holier among us may strive for beatitude – a state of supreme and blessed happiness. The more happy-go-lucky will settle for a feeling of *joie de vivre* – experiencing a lasting optimism and sense of enjoyment. However, the gates of Elysium are usually closed and we have to content ourselves with short-term delight.

TABLE 8.3

A GUIDE TO PROVIDING CUSTOMERS WITH EMOTIONAL SUPPORT

Emotion	Typical Indicators	Support Mechanisms
Anger – a feeling of outrage, bitterness or indignation caused by a perceived wrong.	– Eyes have penetrating stare, lids are tense. Brows likely to be lowered and drawn together. Lips are pressed together or opened and pushed forward. Speech is staccato-like and pitched at higher or lower level than the norm.	– Allow customers to express their anger (in a civilised manner) before attempting to respond. Listen and then rephrase comments of customer in a neutral manner. Attempt to convince customers that the cause of their anger will be dealt with by a specified date. Alternatively, help them to change their perception of the situation, convincing them that their anger was unnecessary.
Anxiety – a feeling of unease, foreboding or concern often associated with indecision.	– Speech patterns marked by stutters, slips of the tongue, over-use of 'um', 'er', 'ah'. Pace of speech is unduly slow. Considerable hand movement and facial twitching.	– Put customer at ease by making time available now or at a specified date. Do not force pace of discussion. State that you understand the dilemma and help customer to work through options and make a decision. Do not make decision for the customer. (cont'd....)

TABLE 8.3
A GUIDE TO PROVIDING CUSTOMERS WITH EMOTIONAL SUPPORT

Emotion	Typical Indicators	Support Mechanisms
Boredom – a feeling of listlessness, lack of interest or enthusiasm.	– If sitting there will be a dropping of the head, body in a leaning backward posture with legs out-stretched. If standing there will be much fidgeting and head movement.	– Stop what you are doing/saying and check cause of boredom – going over familiar ground, mis-interpretation of customers' needs, using jargon unfamiliar to the customer. Once cause has been identified, change approach. Avoid being reproachful.
Confusion – a feeling of puzzlement and agitation, of being in two minds about a situation.	– Appears agitated, distracted. Exhibits a questioning look with furrowed brow.	– Find out the cause of the confusion, prompting the customer where necessary. Recognise that the individual wants to find a way out of the predicament. Present the options and where possible provide an opportunity for a subsequent change of mind to take place with-out penalising the customer.

(cont'd...)

TABLE 8.3

A GUIDE TO PROVIDING CUSTOMERS WITH EMOTIONAL SUPPORT

Emotion	Typical Indicators	Support Mechanisms
Grief – a feeling of sadness resulting from the loss of a valued person or animal.	– Brows raised, upper eyelids lowered, mouth down-turned.	– Share the grief by encouraging the customer to express his/her feelings. Do not show embarrassment at crying or sobbing. Do not rush the encounter, nor decision taking.
Guilt – a feeling of remorse and responsibility for having committed an action which conflicts with one's values and beliefs.	– Flushed appearance, avoidance of eye contact, speaking at a very low volume.	– Do not condone cause of guilt unless it is the result of a genuine mistake. Encourage individual to acknowledge their guilt and seek their commitment to its non-recurrence.
Embarrassment – a feeling of diffidence or humiliation in dealing with a situation.	– Blushing, halted speech, eyes focused downward, hands open and brushing body.	– Exude warmth and compassion. Find out cause of embarrassment and offer to work with person in removing it. Where possible re-assure customer that the feeling is 'normal'. Do not simply pass it off without some guidance on how to avoid its recurrence. (cont'd...)

TABLE 8.3
A GUIDE TO PROVIDING CUSTOMERS WITH EMOTIONAL SUPPORT

Emotion	Typical Indicators	Support Mechanisms
Fear – a feeling of alarm or dread which may be irrational, provoked by past experience or the unknown.	– Raising and drawing together of brows. Eyes open and tense; mouth open and lips drawn back tightly. Possible shaking of the hands. Speech higher pitched than normal but volume low.	– Establish the cause of the fear. Where possible allay the feeling by calm reassurance and highlighting that the type of fear is not un-common and has been overcome in similar situations.
Frustration – a feeling of annoyance or exasperation at not achieving an objective or satisfying a need.	– Tense eyes. Speech louder than usual. Fists clenched and may be used to punch the table.	– Frustration arouses aggression – listen to the content of the cus-tomer's comments and ignore the the emotion surrounding them. Calm the customer before attempt-ing to deal with the core issue. Where possible offer a substitute goal or satisfy an alternative need to give a sense of achievement.

(cont'd...)

TABLE 8.3
A GUIDE TO PROVIDING CUSTOMERS WITH EMOTIONAL SUPPORT

Emotion	Typical Indicators	Support Mechanisms
Resentment – a feeling of ill-will or grudge arising from a situation where one perceives oneself to have been placed at a disadvantage or slighted.	– Similar to anger but marked by tendency to remain silent with lips clenched accept for deep exaggerated sighs.	– Find out cause of resentment and deal with bolstering self-esteem before seeking ways of resolving the situation. If cause is unjustified help customer to recognise and admit it without loss of face.
Impatience – a feeling of restiveness at the pace of a process or person in meeting one's needs or goals.	– Fidgeting, abruptness of speech, loud sighing, tapping surface with fingers.	– Acknowledge presence of customer as soon as possible. Give time indication of meeting customer's needs. Explain reasons for delay. Offer options and trade-offs for shortening time spans to completion. Remain calm.

There is a ladder of delight which, being normal humans, our customers want to climb. Any help in ascending the ladder is much appreciated; action which causes a fall from the desired rung is rarely forgotten nor forgiven.

The first step on the ladder of delight is contentment, subsequent rungs are:

- Gratification.
- Joyfulness.
- Jubilation.
- Exhilaration.
- Exultation.
- Ecstasy.

Contentment is an emotional state which is the outcome of satisfaction with the way in which objectives or needs have been met. It signifies that there are no grounds for complaint; the outcome is what the customer expected.

Gratification is a more positive emotional state resulting from an outcome which has in some way exceeded expectations, and merits acknowledgement of the person who has contributed to the outcome. This acknowledgement may be little more than a 'thank you'; other visible signs of low level delight may not be apparent to the service provider.

Joyfulness, on the other hand, can not easily be hidden from view. It is the emotional state in which we communicate to others our sense of delight at the outcome of some event which significantly exceeded our high expectations.

Jubilation occurs when we share our joyfulness with others. It may take the shape of a celebration to mark an event which has significance for a group which is linked by similar characteristics. It is possible for a service provider to create the conditions for jubilation at such events as a wedding reception or among passengers flying on a traditional holiday. Carnivals and sporting events are situations in which companies can and do create occasions for jubilation through sponsorship and corporate hosting.

Exhilaration is both a physical and emotional state. It has its source in a thrilling experience which exposed the individual to an uncommon situation which created feelings of stimulation of various organs, particularly the heart. A voluntary exposure to danger, real or imaginary, can heighten exhilaration, whether caused by skiing or riding on a roller coaster. Care has to be taken to avoid damage to a customer through over excitement; springing surprises on customers who are young or very old can negate delight. However, used with discretion and safety, opportunities to exhilarate exist in travel, hotel and retail industries. Stimulation through simulation will provide increasing opportunities to delight.

The next two rungs on the ladder of delight are likely to prove to be out of reach for most manufacturers and providers of services. Nevertheless, it is useful to bear them in mind as real, though remote, possibilities.

Exultation is a state of rejoicing to the total exclusion of all else. It is brought about by some emotionally laden event, often of a quasi-spiritual nature in contrast to the physical basis of exhilaration. Exultation is usually associated with a life change, such as surviving a major operation. It can also result from escaping from a dangerous situation, and is therefore a state of delight which has to be handled sensitively by the providers of such services as personal security.

Ecstasy is the most exalted form of delight. It is the stuff of souls, and therefore outside the province of industry and commerce. It might be argued that drugs can be manufactured and conditions created where ecstasy is experienced by 'customers'. In such cases those believing they have had an ecstatic experience are living in a fool's paradise, and not in the realm of delight.

There are two types of delight to be avoided in customer care: euphoria and *schadenfreude*. Euphoria is delight based on some misconception. Born of over-confidence or over-optimism, it leads an individual into a false sense of delight which comes to an abrupt and often painful end when the cause of delight is discovered to be illusory. The outcome of false promises and over-hyped expectations, euphoria will eventually destroy those who debase the coinage of delight.

Schadenfreude is an emotional state which reveals the dark side of delight. It depends for its existence in taking joy in the misfortune of others. Gloating and spite are the bedfellows of *schadenfreude*, and together they smother whatever true joy lies in their way.

Any ladder of delight which has rungs for euphoria and *schadenfreude* will cause a mighty fall for those who venture on them. In this book the aim is to ensure that the rungs are solid and secure and that the first three or four can be climbed by anyone seeking to help customers benefit from the Delight Factor.

The trouble with the ladder of delight is that the rungs are not evenly spaced – the distance between them lengthens as one ascends. To move up even one rung calls for the stimulation of the gamut of positive emotions. How this can be done is shown in Table 8.4. This also lists indicators of success. This is the great advantage of delight, that you can see, hear, and feel it working on your customers.

Conclusion

Science is revealing more insights into the causes and consequences of our sensory and emotional make-up. We know more than our ancestors how senses and emotions can be combined in many ways to create a sense of delight. Sustaining that sense, replicating it day-in and day-out, calls for a whole new field of management. Why this should be so and how it can be brought about are the subjects for the next chapter.

TABLE 8.4
STIMULATING EMOTIONS OF DELIGHT

Emotion	Stimulators	Indicators of Success
Amazement – a feeling of intense pleasant surprise in confronting the unexpected.	– Meet 'secret' wish. – Provide a physically thrilling experience. – Provide unexpected device to resolve a situation. – Provide opportunity to significantly enhance life-style. – Provide a totally new perspective to a situation.	– Positive response to situation, display of joy. – Willingness to repeat the experience and/or share it with others. – Acceptance of the solution. – Opportunity grasped. – Perspective welcomed and acted upon.
Amusement – a feeling of pleasure from being entertained in a manner which appeals to one's sense of humour.	– Presenting a diversion which is enjoyable. – Reducing or removing tension from a situation by introducing humour. – Presenting a product or event in a manner that results in desired mirth.	– Expression of appreciation verbally or physically. – Reduction in tension. – Laughter or appreciative chuckles.

(cont'd...)

TABLE 8.4
STIMULATING EMOTIONS OF DELIGHT

Emotion	Stimulators	Indicators of Success
Approval – an expression of endorsement of a person, situation or course of action.	– Presentation which is sensitive to the values and beliefs of the customer. – Seeking needs and expectations of customer and responding to them.	– Praise from customer. – Recommendation by customer to others.
Bliss – a feeling of total contentment, especially associated with marriage.	– Provision of desired degree of privacy. – Creation of an ambience which is conducive to complete relaxation.	– Privacy totally respected. – No changes sought by customer despite being genuinely offered.
Comfort – a sense of ease and satisfaction.	– Provision of space, furniture, equipment which are conducive to accomplishing a task in a pleasant manner. – Provision of music and surroundings which lull the senses to a degree desired by the customer.	– Customer is totally relaxed. – Customer returns.
Elation – a feeling of release of high spirits.	– Providing legitimate stimulants for celebrating a significant event.	– Expression of intense pleasure by customer.

(cont'd...)

TABLE 8.4
STIMULATING EMOTIONS OF DELIGHT

Emotion	Stimulators	Indicators of Success
Enthusiasm – a feeling of zest and keeness to participate in an activity or achieve a goal.	– Setting of achievable, though searching, goals with a worthwhile pay-off. – Providing a set of beliefs which are inspirational. – Allowing entry to what is perceived to be an elite club. – Enabling participation in a worth-while cause.	– Goal achieved which meets or exceeds expectations. – Continuing commitment. – Continuing membership. – Active participation.
Excitement – a feeling of arousal of the senses arising from expectation of an imminent pleasurable event.	– Stimulation of expectancy by 'trailing' event. – Advertising. – Providing excerpts of forthcoming event.	– Customers state event met or exceeded expectations.
Friendliness – a feeling of affection for and sympathy with other people.	– Smiling. – Providing signs of preparedness and welcome. – Conveying willingness to meet special needs.	– Smile mirrored by customer. – Customer relaxed. – Customer confirms needs have been met. (cont'd....)

TABLE 8.4
STIMULATING EMOTIONS OF DELIGHT

Emotion	Stimulators	Indicators of Success
Happiness – a cluster of feelings signifying high level of contentment and cheerfulness.	– Signs of anticipating customer's needs and expectations. – Create an ambience which encourages conviviality.	– Body language of customer. – Verbal expressions of total satisfaction.
Pleasure – an intense feeling of gratification resulting from self-fulfilment and/or sharing the delight of others.	– Provide a sense of luxury appropriate to the standards desired by the customer. – Prevent intrusions which could reduce the total enjoyment of the customer.	– Expression of customer satisfaction. Requests no changes when given opportunity for them. – Complete absence of intrusions.

Chapter 9

Managing the Delight Factor

Introduction

Evoking the Delight Factor is not a matter of chance, it is a matter of choice. As we have seen in earlier chapters, delight is caused by the unexpected presence of the desirable, or by the unexpected absence of the undesirable. It is not a constant experience – moments of delight are like hillocks of joy which embellish an otherwise flat and uninteresting landscape. Using a more human analogy, delight experiences are the high points recorded on the cardiograms of every individual's life. Each cardiogram is unique but tends to conform to a general pattern. The aim of managing the Delight Factor is to adapt the generalised pattern to the individual circumstances of the customer.

The Road to Delight Management

In this chapter, the focus is on more specific aspects of managing the Delight Factor. To do this it may be helpful to summarise the main points concerning the Delight Factor which have been outlined so far:

- Delight is a psychological state of temporary pleasure; it is the spiritual essence of customer care. The extent to which that spirit is released depends upon the ability of service provider to manage the Delight Factor.
- The ability to manage the Delight Factor depends upon a number of pre-conditions existing in a company:

- A service quality system (see James J. Lynch's *The Psychology Of Customer Care*, Macmillan,1992, for details of such a system).
- A redefinition of the 'customer'.
- A fresh look at the context in which customers are served.
- A re-shaping of customers' perceptions.
- A recognition of the importance of process as well as outcomes.

- The 'New Customer' is a seeker of three things:
  - Solutions.
  - Time.
  - Delight.

- In striving to provide delight it is essential to recognise its characteristics:
  - It is a temporary state which needs frequent replenishing.
  - It can be experienced both psychologically and physically.
  - It is observable.
  - It can be reinforced by being shared.

- In developing the Delight Factor, the service provider must keep in mind five value clusters:
  - Ethical awareness.
  - Economic vision.
  - Ecological responsibility.
  - Social sensitivity.
  - Personal fulfilment.

- These values influence customers' perceptions of the Delight Factor, as do three other phenomena:
  - Discretionary purchasing power.
  - Discretionary time.
  - Discretionary behaviour.

- All companies can learn something about delight from the hedonistic industries whose prime purpose is to entertain. They reveal the use of a five-stage delight process:
  - Arousing interest.
  - Engaging attention.
  - Evoking absorption.
  - Transforming the experience.
  - Transcending the expected.
- Transplanting the process to other industries can be done by the use of:
  - Metaphor.
  - Geography.
  - Design.
- Purveyors of pleasure fall into three categories:
  - Life exploiters.
  - Life diverters.
  - Life enhancers.

Non-hedonistic industries can learn both negative and positive lessons from each category.

- Customers contribute to their hedonistic experience by effectively playing roles such as:
  - Passive receptor.
  - Solo participant.
  - Team participant.
- Managers and staff need to develop a range of competences for managing the hedonistic experience. For managers these are:
  - Empowerment.
  - Evangelising.

- Trend scanning.
- Opportunity mapping.

For staff the competences are:

- Needs anticipation.
- Expectations gate-keeping.
- Perception-shaping.
- Time-shaping.

- Ways in which delight is blocked include:
  - Blame.
  - Dominance.
  - Idealisation.
  - Normality.
  - Objectivity.

- The use of 'nudges' plays a key role in moving the customer from a state of satisfaction to a state of delight.
- Creating a sense of delight requires the ability to play on all five senses and influence a wide range of emotions. Three emotional states of great importance are:
  - Anxiety.
  - Embarrassment.
  - Happiness.

This summary brings us to the point at which we can analyse the fundamentals of managing the Delight Factor.

A New Field of Management

Hitherto there have been three broad fields in which the traditional skills of management (planning, organising, controlling, motivating, etc.) have been applied: administration, production and providing services. What now is becoming more prevalent is 'Experience Management' – ensuring that the customer enjoys the type of experience he or she is paying for.

'Experience Management' requires five clusters of competence:

- Making the ethereal more tangible.
- Extending the ephemeral.
- Delivering the promise.
- Continual refocusing.
- Serial caring.

Much of delight is ethereal – light and delicate. Making desirable experiences more real calls for a delicacy of touch, a sensitivity to the moods and perceptions of the customer. This, in turn, requires the application of the competences discussed in Chapter 6. Delight does not flower in an atmosphere of obsequious attention, forced jollity, or over-bearing familiarity any more than it will in a climate of rudeness or indifference. The ethereal can be made more tangible by performing a simple act of care, by giving the customer added-value in both its psychic and physical forms. Much of this can be achieved through the selective choice of windows – opportunities for delight – described in Chapter 6 and the nudges listed in Chapter 7.

We saw in Chapter 2 that delight is ephemeral. The longer one can extend the time-span the more delighted the customer will be. This calls for the ability to get rid of any unnecessary anxieties and avoidable embarrassments being endured by the customer by the means described in Chapter 8. In addition, extending the ephemeral requires an avoidance of delays, interruptions and sudden endings of transactions. Much can be gained by applying the techniques of 'time-shaping' outlined in Chapter 2.

Delivering promises is often a custom more honoured in the breach than in the observance in traditional fields of management. This cannot be allowed to be the case in managing the Delight Factor. Creating realistic expectations, ensuring that neither party is deluding the other, and giving fair warning of changes in circumstances are all part of delivery promise. Of particular importance in this aspect of managing the Delight Factor is the five-stage process mentioned in this chapter and described more fully in Chapter 6.

Continual refocusing is necessary for dealing with the law of diminishing delight which can occur when over-reliance is placed on providing only one type of Delight Factor. As we shall see shortly, there are many types of Delight Factor which can be used over time, keeping fresh the customer's sense of delight. By continually refocusing on different types of Delight Factor it is possible to determine the efficacy of each in relation to different customers. Ringing the changes will give rise to peals of delight. Identifying windows of opportunity, and nudging and working on different combinations of the emotions and senses, all described earlier, are the tools for continual refocusing.

What the manager of the Delight Factor is seeking is the 'Lego Effect'. More than 110 billion of these tiny plastic bricks have been sold since 1949, making it the world's favourite toy and giving delight to millions. Part of its success is that it allows children to create their own delight experience, as well as constructing specific models. According to the manufacturer, Lego bricks can be combined in 102,981,500 ways, each combination resulting in delight. Using Lego as a model, in more senses than one, the manager of the Delight Factor needs to be constantly refocusing on new combinations of the physical and the psychological which will create a new Delight Factor.

Serial caring is about providing the customer with what appears to be a seamless robe of delight. From first contact to complete fulfilment and delight, the customer must be made to feel a consistency of care no matter with whom he or she is dealing with in the company. Particularly important here is the avoidance of the anxiety and embarrassment described in Chapter 8.

Making the ethereal more tangible, extending the ephemeral, delivering the promise, continual refocusing, and serial care are not fancy new labels for old practices, but new essentials of management. These new essentials are not intended to supplant traditional management disciplines, but rather they will augment them for the benefit of customers hoping to experience the Delight Factor.

Typology of Delight Factors

There are about twenty types of Delight Factor from which service providers can choose. In broad terms they can be classified as:

- Sensual.
- Emotional.
- Spiritual.

In each category there are types of delight which have their source in the darker side of human nature. These negative Delight Factors are mentioned here both as warning of what to avoid and an avowal that such types have no place in the armoury of respectable companies.

The thread which links different types of negative delight is taking enjoyment in the abuse of self or others. Examples of negative delights are given in Table 9.1. It is not intended as an exhaustive list; each reader may have secret additions to make.

Turning to the brighter side of human nature, Table 9.2 lists a variety of Delight Factors. Examples and points to watch on managing each factor are given. Once again the list is not exhaustive, but by combining different factors it provides many ways to delight customers.

Conclusion

The purpose of this book is to carry customer care across new frontiers of management. As with its sister book, *The Psychology of Customer Care*, it is intended to stimulate new thinking rather than focus on existing practices which by definition are outdated.

Some of the concepts may not apply to specific industries, others may not appeal, but the book will have succeeded if it makes you ask, and helps you answer, the vital question: 'How can I delight my customers today?'

TABLE 9.1
NEGATIVE DELIGHT FACTORS

Sensual

Over-indulgence	– delight stemming from excessive eating, drinking and squandering of money.
Hallucinogenic	– delight arising from the use of drugs to create desired images and sensations through sensory distortion.
Physical abuse	– delight derived from inflicting pain on self or others.

Emotional

Sycophantic	– delight derived from receiving recognition of others at the expense of losing self-dignity.
Gloating	– delight stemming from smug pleasure in the distress of others.
Exploitative	– delight in taking unfair advantage of the weakness or unfortunate circumstances of others.

Spiritual

Schadenfreude	– delight taking satisfaction in the misfortune of others.
Forbidden	– delight which has its roots in breaking laws, flouting conventions for its own sake.
Zero sum	– delight arising from gaining at the expense of others.

TABLE 9.2
POSITIVE DELIGHT FACTORS

Sensual Factors	Examples	Points to Watch
Delight of the new.	– New products. – New combinations of food. – New ways of experiencing sensory gratification. – New clothes. – New service delivery systems.	– Novelty in content, presentation and approach creates delight when providing added-value either psychic or physical. Novelty for its own sake will have little positive appeal to customers. For this delight factor to work it is necessary for the customer to experience or perceive some benefit.
Delight of discovery.	– Finding a different way of doing things. – Finding hidden talents in oneself. – Finding a previously unknown restaurant, product or sensation.	– This factor differs from the novelty one in that the source of delight may have existed for a long time, unknown to the customer. Providing reliable help in making the discovery lies at the heart of this 'Delight Factor'.

(cont'd...)

TABLE 9.2
POSITIVE DELIGHT FACTORS

Sensual Factors	Examples	Points to Watch
Delight of the fulfiled promise.	– Goods delivered on time. – Service delivered as promised or better. – Product performs as specified or better.	– Reliability and reassurance are two potent ingredients in any 'Delight Factor'. Under-promising and over-delivering is a very powerful delight factor.
Delight of the enhanced.	– Experience or product is better than expected. – Incremental but perceptible improvement in a product or service.	– Positively exceeding expectations provides a delight factor which results in the customer being nudged from satisfaction to delight.
Delight of the extended.	– Widening range of products and services.	– Adding to the core product or service peripherals which the customer wants and perceives as congruent is an effective 'Delight Factor', providing customers are forewarned of any subsequent reduction in the product/service range.

(cont'd...)

TABLE 9.2
POSITIVE DELIGHT FACTORS

Sensual Factors	Examples	Points to Watch
Delight of the familiar.	– Consistency in product/service quality. – Maintenance of desired and remembered ambience.	– Nostalgia is an emotional state often triggered by a sensual experience. Familiarity can breed content, hence the popularity of revivals in entertainment. Care needs to be taken to avoid pseudo-familiarity such as covering wooden surfaces with wood-like plastic.
Delight of the vicarious.	– Taking friends to dinner. – Taking children to the circus. – Providing easy access for the less abled.	– This 'Delight Factor' only works if the customer's target audience shows delight, either by eating with gusto everything offered, clapping enthusiastically, or simply being free of anxiety.
Delight of recovery.	– Restored to health. – Return of lost property. – Damaged products replaced. – Damaged relationships restored.	– This 'Delight Factor' will only work if the customer perceives the recovery process to be genuine and fast moving.

(cont'd....)

TABLE 9.2
POSITIVE DELIGHT FACTORS

Sensual Factors	Examples	Points to Watch
Delight of the simple.	– Clear instructions. – Easy to operate controls. – Easy to open packaging.	– The term 'customer friendly' is over-used since it is often based on the provider's perception of what this means. By ensuring that simplicity is based on customers' needs and perceptions this 'Delight Factor' will ensure competitive advantage.

TABLE 9.2
POSITIVE DELIGHT FACTORS

Emotional Factors	Examples	Points to Watch
Delight of surprise.	– Giving an award for customer loyalty. – Reducing price. – Adding peripherals.	– This factor is more than exceeding expectations. It works best when there are no expectations. It is important that the surprise is perceived as a positive one by the recipient and is sprung in a manner which avoids embarrassment.
Delight of relief.	– Finding scarce product in stock. – Ambience comfortable both mentally and physically. – Fears prove unfounded.	– Being put at ease is an effective delight factor. It is essential that the customer does not feel that relief could have come sooner. Care needs to be taken to avoid shock caused by the timing or manner of relief.
Delight of winning.	– Running a raffle. – Allowing the customer to benefit from a small mistake.	– A sense of justified elation at scoring a small victory is a little used delight factor. It needs to be handled in a manner which cannot be perceived as patronising. Any 'prize' should be worth receiving, however small.

(cont'd...)

TABLE 9.2
POSITIVE DELIGHT FACTORS

Emotional Factors	Examples	Points to Watch
Delight of reciprocation.	– Providing customer with a symbol that his/her custom is valued. – Buying supplies (however small) from customers.	– The mirroring of positive feelings can greatly enhance the effectiveness of the 'Delight Factor'. Furthermore giving business such as buying newspapers, sandwiches and stationery from local shops creates a strong bond.
Delight of synchronicity.	– Wedding arrangements run smoothly. – Travel and accommodation arrangements well co-ordinated. – Dinner dance well paced.	– Several things happening at the same time and in accordance with customer needs calls for careful planning and coordination. The key here is to anticipate pit-falls, and thus prevent their occurrence.
Delight of impulse.	– Display of goods which will stimulate and satisfy legitimate self-indulgence. – Provision of goods at an unlikely location, e.g., videos, flowers and sandwiches at petrol stations.	– This factor needs to satisfy impulse without engendering post-indulgence guilt. Care needs to be taken to avoid rash purchases which the customer cannot afford.

(cont'd...)

TABLE 9.2
POSITIVE DELIGHT FACTORS

Spiritual Factors	Examples	Points to Watch
Delight of helping.	– Enabling customer to contribute to a good cause. – Encouraging customer to help in an emergency. – Asking customer to share concern for the 'needy'.	– Genuineness lies at the heart of this 'Delight Factor'. There must be a complete absence of any feeling of being exploited or 'taken for a mug'.
Delight of reconciliation.	– Enabling customer to restore relationship with the service provider which had broken down through the fault of the customer. – Allowing customer access to services from which he/she was formerly banned for non-compliance or default.	– It is important not to make the offending customer eat humble pie. By bolstering self-esteem and making clear the basis of reconciliation the customer can be changed from critic to advocate by the use of this 'Delight Factor'.
Delight of renewal.	– Providing a sense of enhanced self-image. – Making the customer feel competent.	– By renewing the spirit of delight this factor can create a new and more promising basis for customer-provider relationship.

(cont'd....)

TABLE 9.2
POSITIVE DELIGHT FACTORS

Spiritual Factors	Examples	Points to Watch
Delight of trust.	– Allowing temporarily cashless customer to pay for goods at a later date. – Allowing the customer the use of a product or service without pressure to buy subsequently.	– This is possibly the most powerful of the 'Delight Factor'. Not only does it bond relationships but it provides a sound insight into the needs and values of the customer.
Delight of openness.	– Giving a full explanation of any incident. – Explaining the reasons for procedures.	– Within the bounds of legal constraints this 'Delight Factor' will lead to a healthy relationship based on mutual self-respect.

Chapter 10

The Seven Secrets of the Delight Factor

Introduction

Randall Duell, who died in 1992, was a pioneer of delight-making. Duell designed the Universal Studios Tours which rival the Disney theme parks in America and elsewhere. In developing the studio tour concept, Duell defined one of the main secrets of delight: in seeking pleasure, people are not so much interested in experiencing the real thing as in what they imagine to be the real thing. Thus the 'studios' visited by tourists are remote from the reality of work-a-day film making, but are in accord with what people generally imagine a movie studio looks like.

Unfortunately, the circumstances in which the Delight Factor operates in the work-a-day world of industry and commerce are far removed from the fantasy world of Disney and Universal Studios Tours. However, although the situation is different, there are similar forces which can be brought into play providing companies are conversant with what might be called 'the seven secrets of the delight factor'. In this final chapter we shall draw together the various threads of delight management which have run through this book, weaving them into a pattern of delight.

The First Secret – Personalise the Experience

Everyone has a self-image, a sense of their worth in this world. For some the image is more optimistic and self-enhancing than for others. Too low a self-image can lead to suicide; too high an image can lead to egocentric madness. Fortunately, most people have a realistic assessment of themselves; they are capable of sustaining the occasional dent to their *amour propre* and they welcome any boost to their self-esteem. One of the most effective boosts is to create a perception of personalised products and services. By personalising the customer's experience you create a sense of 'just for you' which quickens the soul and makes the individual more open to feelings of delight.

Personalised mementos, such as pencils, books or matches and playing cards, have been common for some time. Computer-based printers spew forth so called 'personal letters' by the thousands. Customers see through this device and its impact can be counter productive, some feeling that their name is being 'abused'. There are, however, ways in which the discreet use of a person's name can evoke delight. For example:

- Table reservation in a restaurant – 'reserved for Mr. and Mrs. X and party'.
- Reserved seats on planes and trains can have a card with the customer's name and some welcoming words.
- Customer choice of music in supermarkets, waiting rooms, or restaurants.
- Customer choice in designating a contribution to charity by a company.

Those who are sceptical as to the importance of personalising an experience should remember that the most frequently sung song is 'Happy Birthday to You'. One reason for this is that the song is always personalised, it enhances self-image and signals celebration – resulting in delight. This gives us a clue to the second secret.

The Second Secret – Delight Breeds Delight

No one sings 'Happy Birthday' by themselves and enjoys it. Although the experience of delight may be confined to one individual, it is sharing delight which can greatly enhance the experience. The delight of a child opening presents on Christmas morning gives delight, however short-lived, to parents and grandparents witnessing the scene. Events associated with life changes, such as christenings, wedding breakfasts and funerals, are usually shared events. On a smaller scale, creating an experience of delight for a customer is likely to be more effective if the customer is able to share it with significant others, such as relatives, friends or peers. In the absence of these, the service provider can create a shared experience by:

- Acknowledgement of the event by as simple a phrase as 'well done', 'aren't you lucky', or 'how I envy you'.
- Discreet exposure of the experience to others – 'come and see what's happened to…'.
- Checking outcomes – 'I'm just phoning to see if you're still delighted with…'.

Care must be taken to avoid embarrassing any of the parties involved in the experience by being over-zealous in bringing about inappropriate sharing; corporate gate-crashing destroys delight. It is necessary to recognise that each individual has his or her distinctive, though not unique, sense of delight. This leads to the third secret.

The Third Secret – What Delights People is What Delights People

The phenomenon of the best selling novel, the block-busting film, and the long running play all testify to the existence of unifying factors in delight which transcend individual differences. Nevertheless, because delight is a function of the senses and emotions, the blend of these factors varies considerably between individuals. It is therefore essential for a company to be aware of the likely 'delight profile' of its customers in order to manage their delight experience effectively. There is, in matters of delight, a four-stage relationship between customer and provider:

- Initiation – at this stage neither party knows the other; Delight Factors should be kept small to avoid the possibilities of misreading the customer.

- Exploration – both parties are getting to know one another, each seeking out experiences which will be mutually beneficial.

- Reinforcement – here the provider uses the data gained in the preceding stages to capture the customer by providing appropriate Delight Factors, both tangible and intangible.

- Symbiosis – when this stage is reached, both customer and provider are aware of their inter-dependency. Even though delight opportunities may be less frequent, their intensity is likely to be greater than in previous stages.

Hotel guests, airline passengers, and bank customers all provide examples of this development of relationships. A first hotel visit, a first flight, or the opening of the first bank account can provide low-key delight experiences which lead to the next stage. Faced with the need to further use the particular service, the customer can choose to begin a new initiation or move into a closer relationship with the provider. If the exploratory phase provides delight, progress to the reinforcement phase is more likely, leading ultimately to the symbiotic relationship of the totally committed customer.

By planning to progress every new customer through all four phases, companies can sketch out 'delight opportunity scenarios' for categories and even individual customers which take full account of their idiosyncrasies and predilections. This knowledge is a great help when it comes to the fourth secret.

The Fourth Secret – Less Can Be More

Earlier in the book emphasis was placed on using nudges rather than pushes to move customers into a state of delight. Recognising the differences between individuals, it is preferable to aim for many small surprises, rather than one large one. A single rose can have a greater impact on the heart than a roomful of flowers.

Although delight experiences can be repeated, a law of diminishing returns applies. Eventually the occasion for joy becomes the signal for a yawn. With each delight experience the expectation threshold of the customer is raised. Controlling the rate of rise of the expectation threshold is a key attribute of managing the Delight Factor.

Delight experiences therefore need to be planned in series rather than individually. The perennial question is not so much 'How do I surprise the customer?', but 'As a consequence of this surprise what will the customer expect next?'. Without an answer to this question, it maybe better not to use the Delight Factor at all. For those who wisely decide to keep the Delight Factor as a major competitive weapon, the next secret will sharpen its cutting edge.

The Fifth Secret – Blend Novelty and Nostalgia

People seek the new and hark back to the old. Much depends on age. When we are young we yearn for the stimulus of innovation; to be at least in the fashion if not ahead of it. As we grow older we search for the reassurance of the familiar, the comfort of previous experiences. However, many such experiences are distorted by history or coloured by the memory. It is important to be aware of these influences in managing the Delight Factor.

Delight experiences can arise from creating situations which are new to the customer or which recreate the past. The combination of trips on Concord and the Orient Express is what might be called a mega-delight experience drawing on both new and old technology. The Delight Factor as described in this book operates on a much smaller scale, though the principle remains the same – new can be blended with old.

This blending need not be expensive; 'old time' courtesy at supermarket check-outs can be blended with a range of new calculating and stacking techniques. A genuinely friendly welcomer at the entrance to a department store can ease a customer's search as swiftly as an escalator. There is a danger of resurrected customer care practices being perceived as tacky and offensive to those cherished but distorted memories.

By the judicious selection of the most appealing of the old with the most innovative, it is possible to create experiences that delight. Looking ahead to the 21st century it is safe to predict that, however sophisticated the technology of toys may become, a robotic Father Christmas is unlikely to provide for the young (and young at heart) the delight of his human counterpart. Over dependence on technology must be avoided as we shall discover with the sixth secret.

The Sixth Secret – Technology Helps and Hinders

Few would deny that technology has made and continues to make a major contribution to the propensity of products and services to delight. From the convenience of the cash dispenser to the various services of telecommunications, mankind as consumer is living in a golden age. But technology, like gold , is soulless. While it would be feasible for a machine to measure the physical indicators of delight, no machine can gauge the extent to which delight can feed the soul and move the spirit.

Machines can excite, stimulate, pacify, or ameliorate, but any customer care strategy which relies solely on technology is likely to lead to robotic responses by both customers and providers.

In planning how best to use technology as a positive force for delight we must bear in mind that customers are purposeful, goal-seeking and fickle. In the chapter 'The New Customer' we saw that those engaged in customer care must satisfy three categories of need: physical, psychological and spiritual. While technology can cope with the first two categories, it needs some degree of human intervention to provide satisfaction of the third.

In terms of goal-seeking, the customer comes not with a single goal but with a variety, each linked to one of the categories of need. It is, therefore, essential for service providers to identify and anticipate customers' goals on a broad front. Traditionally, customer goals have focused on price and quality. Technology has done much to lower prices and raise quality standards. The 'New Customer' now virtually takes for granted that his or her economic and performance goals will be similarly satisfied by a range of competitors.

Price and performance being similar, companies have to deal with the third characteristic of customers – their fickleness. Tomorrow they will want something different from what they wanted today. They change their minds on priorities, and in the very development of an activity towards a particular goal they may begin to desire a different one. For this reason there needs to be some human interaction in assessing customers' needs, helping them to meet their goals, and responding to their changes of mood. Technology by itself can blind providers to the changing customer. No cash dispensing machine, however efficient, can assess the attitude of the customer to the bank at a particular point in time.

Machines can create delight, but they can not experience it. Experiencing delight is the prerogative of humankind. Which brings us to the last secret.

The Seventh Secret – There is No End to Delight

In biblical terms it could be claimed that Adam and Eve lived in a garden of delight from which they were expelled. As a consequence, a continuing state of delight was replaced by limited opportunities to experience it. Coming down to earth, this book is concerned with keeping customers satisfied rather than re-inventing Eden.

Because it is part of the human condition, the limits to delight are bound only by human potential. There are in fact no known limits. The opportunities to evoke delight are as varied as the opportunities to show care. These can range from the exercise of highly professional skills to as small a gesture as holding open a door. A look, a touch, or a helping hand are all instruments of delight.

Conclusion

The last decades of the 20th century have witnessed the growth of quality consciousness and customer power. Consumer legislation, international quality standards, and competition based on customer care are as much shapers of industry and commerce as were in their time mass production, mass marketing and computer technology.

As we progress into the 21st century these instruments of change will be blended with others to enable most companies to claim justifiably that their products are high quality and their customer care practices are innovative. A few companies in the vanguard of their industries will be able to claim something better: not only do they serve and care for their customers – they delight them. Such companies are bound to be winners.

Index